& share your knowledge
Lisa Beth

RAISE YOUR GAME, NOT YOUR VOICE

HOW LISTENING, COMMUNICATING, AND STORYTELLING SHAPE COMPLIANCE PROGRAM INFLUENCE

LISA BETH LENTINI WALKER AND STEF TSCHIDA

right message, right time!
Stef

Raise Your Game, Not Your Voice: How Listening, Communicating, and Storytelling Shape Compliance Program Influence is published by CCI Press, an imprint of CCI Media Group, Dallas, Texas

Copyright © 2021 by Lisa Beth Lentini Walker and Stef Tschida

All rights reserved. No part of this publication may be reproduced, distributed, or transmitted in any form or by any means, including photocopying, recording, or other electronic or mechanical methods, without the prior written permission of the publisher, except in the case of brief quotations embodied in critical reviews and certain other noncommercial uses permitted by copyright law.

ISBN: 978-1-7350285-3-8

Editor: Emily Ellis

Designer: Sam Kerner

Author Photo: Rachel Seifert and The Merry Hour

CCI Media Group
www.corporatecomplianceinsights.com

CONTENTS

Introduction	1
About the Authors	3
Chapter 1: Becoming a Deep Scholar in Your Organization	**5**
What It Means to Be a Scholar	6
Characteristics of the Best Scholars	9
6 Steps to Becoming an Organizational Scholar	12
5 Ways to Master Scholarship Within Your Role	18
Chapter 2: Intentional Relationship Management: Manage Your Relationships Like a BOSS!	**22**
5 Types of Stakeholders and How to Engage with Each	25
5 Actions to Cultivate More Positive Relationships	32
3 Relationship-Destroying Actions to Avoid	35
Chapter 3: Audience Dynamics: Winning Others Over in the Maelstrom	**42**
LAUNCH: Learning a New "Language"	43
5 Tactics to Match Your Phrasing to the Audience's	45
Motivational Interviewing	46
Chapter 4: Understand Your Organization's Communications Approach	**51**
Study How the Company Currently Communicates	52
Get Input from Across the Company	56
Understand How Your Content Benefits Others	58
Learn How to Partner with Corporate Communications	61
7 Steps to Build Your Relationship with the Communications Team	63
How to Communicate in the Absence of Communications Support	66
Chapter 5: The Storyteller's Secrets	**68**
Why do stories have such an important role in conveying information?	69
The Neuroscience Behind Effective Storytelling	73
3 Tips for Crafting an Effective Story	77
Types of Stories	80
What if I don't have my own stories?	82
Chapter 6: Right Message, Right Audience, Right Time	**88**
5 Key Publications Milestones	91

Chapter 7: Say It Again: Repetition Matters   **95**
   Learning Styles: Different People Learn Differently   98
   How to Vary Your Message   101

Chapter 8: The Listening Advantage: The Gift of Feedback   **106**
   Feedback Is a Gift of Time and Energy   107
   4 Ways to Mitigate Risks and Maximize Opportunities Associated with 2-Way Dialogue   108
   The Numbers Don't Lie   111
   Seek Out the Voice of the Customer   113
   Gathering Voice of the Customer Feedback   117

Conclusion   **119**

Acknowledgements   **121**

Worksheets   **125**
   Events Roadmap   126
   Understanding Your Organizational Brand   128
   Initial Interview About Compliance at the Organization   130
   Personal Stakeholder Map   132
   Engaging with Your Stakeholders   134
   Motivational Interviewing and Gaining Buy-In   138
   Communication Channels Checklist   140
   Why My Message Matters   142
   Preparing to Meet with Corporate Communications   144
   Getting Your Message Out   146
   Developing Your Storytelling Narrative   148
   Balancing Stakeholder Needs with Compliance Goals   150
   Content Creation Checklist   154
   Content Approval Checklist   155
   Content Publication Checklist   156
   Ongoing Voice of the Customer Ideas   158
   Identifying the Core Concepts of Your Message   160
   Planning for Repetition: Audience Variation   161
   Planning for Repetition: Channel and Format Variation   162
   Feedback: Tracking Data   164
   Planning for Feedback: Response Plan   166
   Gathering Voice of the Customer Feedback   168

INTRODUCTION

Have you ever been at a social event with a loud crew of revelers? When you have a gathering, each knock at the door often adds to the volume in the room as people, happy to see each other, communicate in varying tones of voice. Perhaps your family takes "being heard" to Olympic sport levels: Each person talks over the other in a race toward decibels that will make your ears ring for hours. While this can be fodder for family lore and great stories of the loudest person in the room, it's usually terrible for truly meaningful and nuanced communication. Striving to be the loudest voice in the room is also not an ideal way to handle communication within an organization.

As two professionals whose careers have spanned legal, compliance, and communications (with lots of overlap), we understand that clear, strategic communication is the key to introducing anything new in an organization—particularly when these changes are significant and impact every area of a company, as is the case when introducing or formalizing a compliance program.

We met in 2012 while working "in the trenches" to respond to terrorism incidents, data breaches, and other chaotic events at a global travel management company. We hit it off immediately, connecting not only on our mutual work, but also on the importance of strong, effective communication being invaluable regardless of someone's role. At the time, we never thought our partnership would culminate almost a decade later with this book, but we're thrilled it has.

Some consider communication a "soft" skill, one that can be pushed to the side when the job gets hard or when you need to drive results. We couldn't disagree more. We have seen firsthand that effective communication aligned with business objectives—and targeted to the audience—has a significant impact on any initiative. This is especially true given the significant amount of transformation so many organizations are navigating as the workplace and business itself continues to change rapidly.

We also know that in this incredibly (and increasingly) technology- and artificial intelligence-driven world, "people skills" are more needed than ever. At the core, those "people skills" are communication skills. As the compliance, ethics, governance, and risk functions continue to grow, develop, and require effective understanding, the communication skills to drive comprehension, alignment, and buy-in are increasingly vital in differentiating the truly effective professional.

Whether you're a practitioner just entering your career, moving to a new organization, or simply looking to hone your communication skills, this book is for you. In the pages that follow, you'll get tools, tips, and resources to establish your status as a scholar within your organization as you build relationships and get the data you need to communicate compelling stories to all stakeholders—when they need it and in the channels where they already consume information. Our intent is ultimately to help you realize your organizational and career goals as a compliance professional within any organization you choose to join. Onward!

ABOUT THE AUTHORS

Lisa Beth Lentini Walker is a seasoned compliance professional and an attorney qualified in New York, New Jersey, DC, and Minnesota. Lisa Beth has worked with leading global organizations to successfully launch, lead, and support compliance programs in an evolving world in which risk management is no longer enough. Along the way, she learned the importance of cultivating strong relationships and the power of great communication to connect people to the organization's vision.

Lisa Beth's daily mantra is "People are at the heart of every great story, and stories are how people remember." She believes that resilient organizations are powered by people and fueled by purpose. Lisa Beth has had the opportunity to work with private and public companies, nonprofits, and professional organizations to put values into action.

A teacher at heart, Lisa Beth has always embraced opportunities to help grow and cultivate future leaders. She is happiest when surrounded by family, friends, and colleagues who want to make a difference and who rejoice in the successes of others. Fortunately, she has been able to combine her love of education, communication, and subject matter expertise into a career that keeps her excited about the art of possibility every day.

Stef Tschida spent 15 years working in all aspects of corporate communications before starting her own communications consultancy. She has supported some of the biggest organizations in some of the most highly regulated industries, but today Stef finds she's most passionate about helping small and mid-sized companies clearly communicate to those who matter most to their success.

Stef's professional motto is, "No stakeholder left behind," and that's exactly the promise she brings to her work. Stef has led public relations, client communications, and internal communications at regional and global levels, so she thinks about all relevant audiences when it's time to communicate information.

Growing up, Stef loved to write her own books, mixing up the first and last names of her friends to form the characters. Ever the communicator, when she found herself in trouble at school, it was always for talking too much. Stef counts herself lucky to have built a career around her innate love of communicating.

CHAPTER ONE

BECOMING A DEEP SCHOLAR IN YOUR ORGANIZATION

"A scholar is committed to building on knowledge that others have gathered, correcting it, confirming it, enlarging it."

– Parker Palmer, author and activist

Before you can even begin to convey your compliance messages, you need to be skilled at navigating your organization to get things done. In fact, it's imperative to really understand your company inside and out. Subject matter expertise is never enough to be truly successful. Compliance professionals must understand their company's unique footprint, culture, and strategy before determining how they'll communicate to grow their program. We call people who are especially successful at this "scholars."

WHAT IT MEANS TO BE A SCHOLAR

Scholars are distinguished by their deep knowledge and expertise in a field. By applying scientific rigor and logic-based inquiry in the search for objective truth, scholars gain a greater understanding of and ability to navigate circumstances and challenges. Scholars have a high aptitude for inquiry-based exploration, a sharp focus on keeping work clearly defined, a strong curiosity to drive them forward in their endeavors, and a desire to question why currently accepted ideas are recognized as truths.

When contemplating communications, taking a methodical and focused approach is crucial. Every organization changes with time; you cannot rest in your acquisition of knowledge, because there are bound to be evolutions in strategy, customer base, employee needs and obstacles, and more. Becoming a scholar means becoming a person who is continually learning.

You should start now to form the habit of regularly studying your organization. In-depth knowledge of the organization serves the scholar well, because:

- **Scholars are navigators.** Just like the early wayfarers who sailed by watching the constellations and then later used compasses or GPS to guide the way, organizational scholars find the patterns and true north of the organization. Understanding the signs, signals, and guideposts allows you to find your way and guide others.

- **Scholars are in-demand resources.** Historians are able to tell stories that resonate with others because they recount examples of similar events and the outcomes. As a scholar, you become an organizational historian and understand the players, outcomes, and lore of the place where you work. As great historians know, *knowledge* of history is not enough; without learning from history, people are doomed to repeat it.

- **Scholars command respect.** Scholars are respected for their deep pursuit of knowledge and command of the material. Just like other scholars, people who work tirelessly to understand and successfully use the information to improve outcomes are to be admired.

A scholar is a trusted and accomplished expert, a creator of knowledge who can integrate disparate data and concepts to innovate and reach new conclusions. You are entering the knowledge business, and the production and evaluation of knowledge are essential to your success.

To become a scholar, you must first understand the driving force of the scholar: a determination to know and be able to represent the organization, as well as to create a foundation for future success. The following chapters will demonstrate how you can use that knowledge to integrate, create, and innovate as a scholar.

Scholarship the Jedi Way

Once I went to an organization where there was a person who called themselves the "Yoda" of the company because of their deep knowledge gained over many years of employment. The reference to a critical character in the Star Wars saga was interesting to me.

In Star Wars, Yoda was a Jedi Master. He trained Jedi Knights, including Luke Skywalker, to connect with and harness the power of the Force. Yoda was a source of deep knowledge about the Force, but he was also a brilliant strategic thinker and facilitator.

As you think about gathering knowledge in your organization, it is important to be able to differentiate between the path of light and the path of darkness. On the Dark Side, the Force is used for destructive and selfish purposes. The path of light is focused on empowerment, good deeds, and noble causes.

As you consider your path toward becoming a scholar in your organization, be careful not to hoard information or become a barrier to progress. Scholars in their truest sense are people who share for the greater good. The true Yoda of an organization challenges convention, helps others to see patterns, acts as a role model and enabler of success, and reflects on an ever-evolving landscape.

As Yoda said, "Mind what you have learned. Save you it can."

–Lisa Beth

CHARACTERISTICS OF THE BEST SCHOLARS

Ethics & Integrity

Ethics and integrity are the core qualities of a successful scholar. Ethical scholars treat their colleagues with respect at all times and are inclusive leaders focused on equity. They are open to feedback and constructive criticism. They don't seek to gain leverage over others through their position or esteem.

A degree of candor in conversation is equally critical to the scholar being perceived as respectfully honest and as a proper assessor of situations. Being an ambassador of your organization's code of ethics (and of your own professional values) will shape the quality of your work and provide a solid foundation for the rest of your career.

It is especially critical for compliance and ethics officers to lead with ethics and integrity; they are generally judged more harshly for perceived ethical inconsistencies.

Persistence

Understanding and navigating the organization can be challenging. How you approach difficulties will have a significant impact on your capacity to respond to them with grit and determination.

A scholar is well aware that some of their pursuits of organizational knowledge will be filled with inconsistencies, change, and divergent pathways. There is never one view of the organization. For example, different units within the same organization may have radically different experiences due to a variety of factors, including leadership, tone from within, and perceptions about the function. Reconciling those diverse perspectives can also be challenging.

Organizational scholars are persistent in the face of these challenges and use them to deepen their understanding of the investigative process in pursuit of an ever-evolving truth.

Scholars, like inventors, often find that new ideas aren't readily accepted. In fact, Thomas Alva Edison once said, "Our greatest weakness lies in giving up. The most certain way to succeed is always to try just one more time." Persistence is being willing to try new methodologies or propose solutions that haven't yet been tried. In the world of compliance, changing behavior and improving culture isn't a one-time endeavor; it is the culmination of persistent effort toward new goals.

Presence

Successful scholars naturally stand out. As they persist in seeking knowledge and listening to others, they are continually identified by their contemporaries as bright and curious. They make others feel comfortable sharing information and find they are requested to contribute to projects for the perspectives they can lend.

A scholar is able to speak with mastery on the topic being discussed. The scholar works to bring clarity and make concepts comprehensible to non-practitioners. They can use storytelling to make complicated subject matter accessible and understandable. By using the language of the organization, the scholar can translate complex concepts and share insights others may miss or misunderstand.

Compliance and ethics officers must also be able to maintain the audience's interest and present information in a way that inspires confidence.

Focus

While scholars need to understand broad trends and the context for their work, they must also manage their time well. Knowing how, where, and when to spend energy is vital to the scholar. They work to maximize efficiency and effectiveness by how they spend their time.

Because of the constraints inherent in the role (resources, etc.), it is critical to prioritize efforts, define achievable goals, and direct energy toward achieving them.

Openness

The most successful scholars keep an open mind to how the organization is shifting and changing, as well as how the world, industry, and competitors are transforming. They consider a wide range of viewpoints regularly, seeking the input of people within and outside the organization to get rich feedback. Scholars not only consider different perspectives, but also possess the humility to know that others may have come to equally valid or superior opinions and solutions. Scholars are willing to modify and adapt as the situation requires.

The best compliance and ethics professionals learn from others. They are not arrogant or self-absorbed, but instead are open to a range of possible solutions and perspectives, which leads to superior outcomes in a diverse and inclusive environment.

Collaboration

The best scholars understand that sustainable impact can't be had from within a vacuum. Collaboration leads to greater buy-in, organizational ownership, and influence within an organization. The best collaborators know how to lead from every seat, making others feel empowered to share and encouraging them to provide the best of their thoughts and efforts. Combining a sense of purpose with their work, collaborative scholars are seen as leaders intellectually and organizationally.

Experienced and successful compliance and ethics professionals have learned that organizations and groups achieve much more by working together toward a common goal than they ever would individually. The wise and successful leader encourages cooperative efforts and is generous and open about recognizing every individual's role in the common success. This encourages open collaboration, loyalty, and trust in those who lead and those who support the enterprise.

6 STEPS TO BECOMING AN ORGANIZATIONAL SCHOLAR

You should be a continuous learner when it comes to your organization. Developing an understanding of the company's ins and outs is critical and requires that you remain nimble. Taking the approach of an investigator or a job applicant every few months will put you in a good position to know what is happening, both in the business and in the industry as a whole. Over time, you'll see changes and developments that can influence how you approach different issues.

To achieve scholarship in your organization, follow these practices:

1. Review your organization's website(s) and public statements regularly.

Foundational information is often provided on an organization's website. One way companies share how they stand out is through their mission or values, which are typically prominently displayed in the "About Us" section. Read closely to learn what might be different about your organization. For instance, look at how the articulated core values are presented to outsiders compared to your experience inside the organization. If one of the core values is sustainability or customer service, that's good to know, but how does it compare to internal messaging or what is rewarded?

Understand the "basics"—like company size, location, and history. Always look at environmental, social, governance, and organizational responsibility/sustainability statements. Find out which groups and causes the organization supports. Be an ambassador and champion of the code of ethics and any other supporting values.

If you are working with a specific subsidiary or product, familiarize yourself with the information presented on the webpages dedicated to that group.

We'll share more about using the company website for effective communication in Chapter 4.

2. Research what the company says and does on traditional and social media.

You should be reading the news that comes up when you Google the organization, but company blogs are also rich sources of information, especially for organizations that are growing or don't have public reporting obligations. You should know what information is taking up air space for the organization and what is getting the most traction and reaction.

LinkedIn is also a good tool for learning about what kind of news the organization communicates—and, therefore, wants you to know. Read leaders' posts and the organization's page on LinkedIn and see what kind of updates are featured.

Check out the organization's other social media channels, such as YouTube, Twitter, Instagram, and Facebook. What's featured, and how is coverage focused (or not)? During your research, be on the lookout for both positive news and examples of challenges you encounter.

Finally, it can be helpful to take a look at reviews of products or experiences—including complaints. You can get a lot of insight about trends through the Better Business Bureau, Google reviews, Glassdoor, and other sources of customer interactions.

Reference Chapter 4 to learn more about studying external channels including social media to understand how your company communicates.

Pro Tip from **Lisa Beth**

Follow, like, and interact with your organization on social media. You will be able to see what is happening in real time. But ALWAYS be honest about who you are and any affiliations you have, and ALWAYS follow the social media policy and your organization's code of ethics.

3. Become a financial sleuth.

If you are working for a public company, you should stay apprised of what the organization shares with investors. For most large companies, you should be able to access and listen to publicly available earnings calls and read any and all filings, including periodic reports, proxy statements, 8-Ks, and more. These are all treasure troves of information about the company, covering a range of topics, from new products and company risks to whether revenue and profits are growing, stable, or declining.

If you're working for a startup, check out the company's profile on Crunchbase, or see if you can get a Dun & Bradstreet report. If you are working for a nonprofit, check out the publicly filed Form 990 and look for reports to donors. In doing so, you can get caught up on rounds of funding, acquisitions, recent hires, charitable contributions, and relevant press coverage.

In addition to understanding financial conditions, it's important to assess the financial health of the organization and the drivers of results. If you don't understand enough of it yourself, set some time with one of the folks on your finance team to have them explain. Asking for help is a sign of strength and a willingness to learn.

4. Get deep into company culture.

You may be able to glean a bit about overall organizational culture through a company's blog and social media accounts, but to really build on that information and get a firm handle on the company culture, dig deeper.

Look for information from internal sources. There are many ways organizations can measure internal perceptions, including getting input from your internal customers. Look for any assessments of company culture, any employee insights, or a "voice of the customer" survey.

Study company communications. Learn all of the industry- and company-specific acronyms. It is often helpful to have a quick guide to acronyms and nuances so you know what they are. When you hear an acronym you don't know, make note of it or ask in the moment for clarification.

It's also critical to study internal documents like sales guides, business unit results and plans, and other communications, including updates on key initiatives. Take a front seat when it comes time for town hall updates and strategic kickoffs.

Pro Tip from **Lisa Beth**

As you learn industry- and company-specific acronyms, if you find that there isn't a ready-made resource to help you remember all the alphabet soup, then start one of your own. When you meet new people, you can share it as a resource and expand upon it over time. Soon you will find that your little guide becomes a must-read, in-demand resource. Plus, it will help the next person on your team assimilate quickly.

5. Gain industry insights.

Aside from knowing as much as possible about your organization, it's a good idea to be able to discuss the industry as a whole. It's even more impressive to be able to talk knowledgeably about competitors and how your organization fits into the bigger picture.

Look up competitors by visiting your company's LinkedIn page and scrolling down to the "Pages people also viewed" section. There should be a few competitors there. Do the same thing with the competitors you find until you have a pretty good sense of the big players in the field. If the company has a Crunchbase page, you should be able to find a list of competitors on its profile as well. The executive compensation overview of a publicly listed company's proxy statement is another good source of information for comparable organizations; check the peer company list for inspiration.

Take some time to read what professional organizations are saying about the industry. Sign up for some professional publications or blogs about the industry or industries your organization operates in.

6. Learn to ask great questions.

When you come into an organization as a new employee, you have fresh eyes. While it can be overwhelming to "drink from the firehose" as you get up to speed, there's value in not knowing anything and, like a child, having to constantly ask "Why?" to understand the world around you.

Unfortunately, in the name of expertise, it's common to stop asking questions and challenging underlying assumptions as your company tenure increases. Great organizational scholars, however, never lose their ability to think critically about the most foundational aspects of their organizations and the industries in which they operate. And, most importantly, they never stop asking questions about why things are the way they are.

There are countless great questions to be asked, but here are some to keep in mind:

- Why does our industry exist? What fundamental problem are we solving for those we serve?
- What does our customer need that we're not providing to them today? Why are we choosing not to address this need?
- What would the world look like if our organization weren't operating? Who would benefit? Who would lose out?
- What forces outside our walls could help us? What external forces could hurt us?

- Who could we partner with to accomplish our goals more easily or more quickly?
- Who aren't we serving that we could be? Why aren't we serving them?

Pro Tip from Stef

Check the internet for videos about the industry or the companies that lead in your space. Sometimes content is easier to consume with a friendly guide or in a different format. Find what works best for you based on your own learning style and preferences.

5 WAYS TO MASTER SCHOLARSHIP WITHIN YOUR ROLE

Being an organizational scholar also means knowing how to navigate communications and your role within the organization. Consider the following as you refine your career and build your communication skills to advance compliance and interact across the organization:

1. Determine how you want to define your role and the value you bring to the conversation.

Start this process by contemplating what your legacy will be within the organization. As you move through your career—whether it is within your current organization, into another company, or closer to retirement—you need to think now about how you wish to be described and what labels you would like others to apply to you. Start first by looking at your job description (or a recent job description) to understand the organization's expectations for your position.

Settle on one or two labels you think are closest to your interests and abilities—ones you would like to be able to apply to yourself. With these labels in mind, you can begin planning your compliance program, how you will communicate, and your own leadership voice within the organization.

2. Create a to-do list to help you become the professional you want to be.

Among other things, your to-do list should feature the activities you are responsible for and initiatives you want to undertake. However, it should include a lot more than just the goals you want to achieve in year one and actions you'll need to take to get there. For instance, by the time you have been with the organization for the first year, you may want to have:

- Taught one or more compliance sessions with key stakeholders in attendance
- Joined a professional association that represents your interests or helped to support your company's membership in key organizations
- Participated in one or more critical initiatives outside of your subject-matter area
- Presented at a meeting of a professional association

3. Find people who can help you achieve your goals.

You will need to have many supporters within your organization; they may take the form of mentors, peer relationships, or other professional connections. Above all, you will need to have key connections in areas like marketing, communications, investor relations, and public relations.

Don't be shy about connecting with colleagues and asking for their support. They will be working with you, so you'll want to develop collaborative and supportive relationships as soon as possible. Ask people you approach to share their proudest moments at the organization so you can understand the kinds of work they've been doing and what inspires them. Ask them about the projects they are most interested in right now to see if anything they're working on is relevant to you and whether it may be something you can help support.

4. Join groups.

Though they vary from organization to organization, there are often a number of formal and informal groups that might be worthwhile to join. These groups are sometimes called employee resource groups (ERG), affinity groups, or volunteer groups, or they may be developed for special projects (e.g., a return-to-work group after a significant disruption). Other options include groups like Toastmasters. Keep your eyes and ears open to learn about them.

You may also see announcements for special events or opportunities offered for employees at the organization. Some of these will be internal, but some may feature outside speakers. They may be fundraisers or other philanthropic events. Attend as many organizational events as you can. You can find out quite a bit about an organization by attending events, and you will likely expand your own professional interests, horizons, and network at the same time.

5. Create a calendar of important dates.

Your company administrative assistants, human resources, communications, investor relations, or public relations teams may have a calendar you can use to keep up with what is happening at the company.

It's important to understand the internal and external events and determine which ones make the most impact on the organizational identity internally and externally. If there isn't already a prepared calendar, make your own and note whether an event is internal or external (or both) using highlighting. See the events roadmap worksheet on page 132 for additional ideas.

As you can see, your job is to be far more than a professional with compliance expertise; it includes serving as a brand translator and scholar of the organization as a whole. Reference the worksheet on page 134 to determine whether you have a sound understanding of your organizational brand.

As a scholar, you'll deliver true value to your organization and your colleagues as a subject matter expert.

CHAPTER TWO

INTENTIONAL RELATIONSHIP MANAGEMENT: MANAGE YOUR RELATIONSHIPS LIKE A BOSS!

"The key to successful leadership today is influence, not authority."

– Ken Blanchard, author and business consultant

Similar to understanding the organization and building your status as a scholar, having strong internal relationships is a prerequisite for communicating effectively. It helps to secure your seat at the table during crises or other significant situations, when things are evolving fast and you could inadvertently get left behind when your expertise is needed the most. This chapter focuses on how to build and maintain strong relationships with stakeholders.

Before we go any further, let's define "stakeholder." *A stakeholder is a person who has an interest in something and who is impacted by and cares about how it turns out.*

They typically:

- Exert influence or pressure to help (or hurt) your program
- Have responsibility for creating change
- Choose to support you and/or the program (or not)
- Benefit or stand to lose something as a result of your work

Compliance and risk is about constant change management. In the twenty-first century, and especially since early 2020, we have been surrounded by constant innovation, regular disruptions, technological changes, and new expectations on a global basis. All of this has created a standard of accelerating and amplified change. What's more, many companies continue to consolidate functions and take advantage of data-driven automation. To effectively handle the increased volume of change and differentiate your compliance program, you must engage your emotional intelligence as a key differentiator.

Change can be categorized as incremental or transformational. Compliance officers are currently in an era of both incremental and transformational change, so it is important to understand the differences and similarities.

Incremental change is typically easier to implement, as it focuses on small improvements to existing processes. In general, incremental change involves fewer changes and a smaller number of impacted stakeholders. An example of incremental change can be something as simple as deciding to substitute fat-free dairy for heavy cream in your coffee, or switching from full caffeine to half-caff. For the compliance officer, incremental change may be an updated policy or procedure; a minor change or edit, it doesn't shift the foundations significantly.

Transformational change, on the other hand, is much more difficult to implement and has a far lower rate of acceptance and organizational success. The more elements subject to change, the greater the likelihood of both significant resistance from a human perspective and that other external factors will impact total operational success.

Transformational change commonly involves altering the "way things have always been," but we humans are creatures of habit: We crave predictability and tend toward reflexive, automatic actions. With transformational change, nothing is automatic, and the brain needs to be rewired—for new expectations and to establish new neural pathways. Any time you have a significant culture change impacting a large number of people, complexity and resistance are guaranteed.

What's more, nearly every organization has been undergoing significant transformational change in the last few years—and that was before the acceleration in remote working. Companies are increasingly embarking on these journeys now; many are being forced to reimagine their business models, distribution methods, and other ways of working to adapt to rapidly changing customer wants and needs.

That's why it's so important for you as a compliance professional to take both types of change into consideration for your compliance program. Because change has become a constant in compliance, communication and relationship building have key roles to play in navigating change. Change management and project management are complimentary but very different skill sets—and both are essential to the compliance officer.

5 TYPES OF STAKEHOLDERS AND HOW TO ENGAGE WITH EACH

Identify each of your stakeholders into their appropriate types:

CHALLENGERS **CHAMPIONS**

NEUTRALS

THE RESISTANCE **THE RESILIENCE**

The Challengers: **ELBOWS-OUT ELLIOT**
(High Influence, Low Support)

Elliot has significant sway within the organization. Elliot doesn't pull any punches with feedback, and oftentimes the commentary can sting. It can feel like bloodsport going in to explain why the program is needed within the organization. Even if you get a good feeling from Elliot in a meeting one day, you shouldn't be surprised if Elliot will throw the program under the bus the next day. These relationships need constant cultivation. You will gain insights into the weaknesses you and/or your program have. Be grateful for the candor, because the Elliots of the world force you to be better and can reveal difficult truths about your program's acceptance within the organization.

Goal: Build support.

How to handle Challengers: Win them over. They are highly influential, but they haven't entirely bought into either you or your program. You will gain good insights and feedback from these folks.

Strategies:

- Find ways to connect on a personal level.
- Connect on professional goals that are aligned with your own (e.g., values and/or outcomes).
- Inquire about and acknowledge concerns.
- Clearly identify how best to communicate with them to engage their support.

The Champions: **LEADER LEE**
(High Influence, High Support)

Lee is also highly influential within the organization and sees what your program brings to the table. Lee won't always be easy to connect with and relate to, but Lee knows that the organization needs your expertise and understands the value of compliance and ethics within the organization. You can count on Lee to help move you and your program forward by providing resources and connections.

Goal: Continue to grow support and properly cultivate their influence in the organization.

How to handle Champions: Gain their sponsorship for the win. They are your culture carriers and may be able to provide you with the resources or expertise you need along the way.

Strategies:

- Connect regularly in a positive and supportive fashion.
- Provide value in the relationship by performing as expected.
- Ask for guidance, feedback, and support.
- Consider mentor relationships if possible.
- Understand their role and responsibilities within the organization and how you can help.

The Resistance: **SIDE-EYE SAM**
(Low Influence, Low Support)

Sam does not like the compliance program and rarely sees the value in it. When compliance topics come up, Sams may passively resist interacting or actively roll their eyes and groan in protest. Sam doesn't hold a ton of sway in the company, but it takes a lot of active power and buy-in to overcome the drag of the Sams in your organization. Sam won't keep you from getting resources, but too many Sams will prevent you from making change.

Goal: Minimize passive and/or aggressive resistance; try to convert The Resistance to The Resilience.

How to handle The Resistance: Gently build bridges. These people may be either passively or actively resisting. They typically have questions or concerns and clearly haven't been won over.

Strategies:

- Determine if this stakeholder represents passive opposition or is more inclined to nefarious resistance.
- Find allies who may be able to help influence and sway the opinions in this group.

- Ask questions to find out why there is low support (e.g., Is it historical activity? Is the perception of compliance compromised?).

- Determine if you are responsible for any of the lack of support and work to remediate or balance any of the erosion of support.

- Be clear about your hopes for the future.

- If you have to go around them, make sure you are transparent in your actions and maintain as much of the relationship as possible.

- Let it go if there is no way you can convert or neutralize. You can't win them all. Don't give up, but be realistic about how much time and effort you expend.

The Resilience: **CHEERLEADER CHARLIE**
(Low Influence, High Support)

Charlie is ready to talk your program up to everyone within earshot. While Charlies may not have a ton of influence within the organization, they believe in you and aren't afraid to say so loudly. Charlies can help provide momentum and a stronger impact for your voice.

Goal: Solidify this base of support.

How to handle The Resilience: Cultivate superfans. These folks are aligned with your vision, goals, and purpose. They want to support you and even play a part in the compliance program's success.

Strategies:

- Connect to fuel the high support you already enjoy.

- Identify their particular skills and talents and how you can leverage them in further support of compliance.

- Recognize their support and thank them.
- Invite them to get involved in supporting initiatives.
- Engage in problem solving so you can win together.
- Ask for input on how compliance can continue to improve and support their initiatives. You can use the worksheet on page 136 to guide this conversation.
- Let them speak up to serve as a cheerleader and supporter, giving them a platform to aid you in influencing.

The Neutrals: **NAT NEITHER**
(Unknown Support, Unknown Influence)

Nat isn't persuaded much in any direction. If you have a Nat here or there, it may not be a concern, but you don't want to have a large number of people who are neither invested nor interested in your program. Nats will generally go along with the majority, so mind where the trends are.

Goal: Assess and educate.

How to handle Neutrals: Shift them for good. These are the people who either don't care or can be easily swayed. Because they are often influenced by other quadrant members, it is important to find a way to move them to a better quadrant.

Strategies:

- Learn more by asking questions about their understanding and perceptions.
- Provide education about your role and the compliance program.
- Ask what you could be doing to gain more support from them.

- Determine how best to move them to a better state.

Once your stakeholders are grouped by type, prioritize stakeholder engagement in the following order:

1. **Champions**
2. **The Resilience**
3. **Challengers**
4. **The Resistance**
5. **Neutrals**

By prioritizing in this way, you start with the highest influence and support, gaining critical momentum before addressing those who are less supportive of you and your efforts.

See the Personal Stakeholder Map on page 138 as an example of how you can track stakeholder engagement and manage those relationships intentionally.

ASSESSMENT OF INFLUENCE

 Strong communication with peers and superiors (including potentially the board of directors)

 Robust interpersonal relationships and networks

 Social astuteness

 Observant and aware of means of communication and buy-in

 Scope of influence (single function, enterprise-wide, board-level, etc.)

ASSESSMENT OF SUPPORT

To discover the stakeholders' support and alignment of interests for the compliance program, discuss and answer the following questions:

What do we hope to achieve in the organization?
What is especially successful about the compliance program?
How will things be better as we start/continue to develop the compliance program?
What do you expect the benefits of the compliance program to be for your work?
What potential consequences or impacts of the compliance program's work can you foresee?

5 ACTIONS TO CULTIVATE MORE POSITIVE RELATIONSHIPS

We all start our relationships the same way: by getting to know each other. But compliance professionals are at a bit of a disadvantage due to perceptions and biases about what the profession does. Terms like "Dr. No," "Bubble Popper," and "Revenue Prevention Department" are tossed around liberally, which means compliance professionals run the risk of starting off any relationship on the back foot.

The best way to counterbalance the "negative pre-appearance press" is to be radically human and authentic. Try these five strategies to foster positive relationships and steer the perception of compliance in the organization toward the positive.

1. Be as transparent as possible.

When you provide information, be clear on what you know, what you don't know, and how you are progressing in any projects you are working on. The people you cultivate relationships with appreciate forthcoming assessments and effective communication. If you can't be transparent because of the sensitivity of an issue, then be clear that you will share as much as you can whenever you can.

2. Remember: Optimism is a North Star.

Whenever you are leading, even in a team of one, you exhibit your own influence and power. People gravitate toward leaders with a "can do" attitude, even if there is a specific path that cannot be taken. It's important to couple optimism with openness to feedback and a lack of bias that welcomes other perspectives. As the compliance person in the room, being a cultural ambassador is critical to fostering the healthy exchange of diverse ideas that makes us all better.

Pro Tip from **Lisa Beth**

Optimism is a choice. My father told me that from the moment I was born, I always looked on the sunny side of life. I was the kid who, when surrounded by mountains of manure, would smile and exclaim, *"There must be a pony here somewhere. Hooray!"*

Some of us aren't born with optimism as a natural characteristic, but we can all cultivate an attitude of optimism. Choose to see the best in others and to look for the hope and opportunities in the challenges you find along the way.

3. Stay connected and engaged with people on a professional and personal level.

Focus on common goals and celebrate achievements. Tell, and more importantly, show people they are valued and that you appreciate the talents and gifts they bring to the organization and to each relationship.

Pro Tip from **Stef**

Connect with colleagues on a personal level. When people know you care about them and are genuinely interested in what matters to them, they'll remember. This has been a hallmark of my career, something I pride myself on. I've continually been amazed at the common ground and connections I've uncovered by spending time with people—even those who are seemingly very different from me. It's a beautiful thing, and its effectiveness for getting the actual work done can't be understated.

Making connections doesn't always feel as urgent as the other items on your to-do list, and it can be tempting to dive right into the meeting agenda or task at hand, but this has proven to be one of the most important ways I've found to get work done.

4. Be transparent and informative up, down, and across the organization.

Provide candid feedback on your compliance program, share the challenges and successes you have had, and be the storyteller for the impact the program has on people.

5. Engage in the 3-O approach: Be open, objective, and observant.

Open: Be visible, available, and interested in all stakeholders. Show deep empathy and check in with people often to provide support and affirm their value.

Objective: Provide opportunities (both formal and informal) for employees to tell their stories, compare their reactions, and express their feelings in a judgment-free zone. You may learn quite a lot from allowing expression, and you'll definitely get more candid feedback.

Observant: Becoming a great scholar of people and their reactions to different approaches is key to fully comprehending their needs and what drives their behavior. Allow for varying personal reactions, and relish the feedback it provides.

By demonstrating that you're open, objective, and observant, you can secure critical feedback and buy-in.

Refer to the visual on pages 42 and 43 for more ideas on building trust and cultivating positive relationships.

3 RELATIONSHIP-DESTROYING ACTIONS TO AVOID

Historically, compliance has been known as a poor partner, a department that doesn't really understand the business. Don't play into the stereotypes. Avoid these negative behaviors in particular.

1. Being an information blocker.

Do not censor information or withhold data. Data hoarders are typically unwelcome in sophisticated companies. To the extent you can, share what information you have, when you have it, even if the information you have is incomplete.

Pro Tip from **Lisa Beth**

While information is power, data hoarders are usually the ones who get caught on the wrong side of the line when things go poorly. Don't believe the fallacy that controlling information is a long-term strategy. At best, data hoarding works for a limited amount of time; ultimately, it sinks a person.

When the end inevitably arrives (usually marked by the end of your role or time with the organization), you will not be seen as a collaborator, and you will have impaired relationships for the long term.

Transparency sets you free.

2. Being a "Debbie Downer" or a "Suzy Sunshine."

Believe it or not, people will look to you as a role model and seek your support and guidance. Aim to be neither completely cynical nor overly optimistic. Strike a reasonable balance and attempt to speak positively when possible.

Pro Tip from **Lisa Beth**

Balance in your perspectives is important. A recent McKinsey report[1] called this important skill "bounded optimism," the

---

[1] D'Auria, Gemma and De Smet, Aaron. "Leadership in a crisis: Responding to the coronavirus outbreak and future challenges." McKinsey & Company, March 16, 2020.
https://www.mckinsey.com/business-functions/organization/our-insights/leadership-in-a-crisis-responding-to-the-coronavirus-outbreak-and-future-challenges

near-magical qualities of calm and confidence, combined with realism.

When I was growing up, my father was an oncologist with a legendary bedside manner. No one wants cancer, but everyone wanted my dad as their doctor if they had it. My dad didn't fill people with false hope; he was clear, concise, and able to outline steps and options, even when they weren't what was hoped for.

Sometimes the options on the table were interventions to preserve or prolong life; other times, they were limited to focusing on core values and priorities while facing very few days ahead. Whether you call it proper bedside manner, bounded optimism, or something else, strike a balance and remain credible at all times.

3. Being inaccessible.

Compliance can't be managed from an ivory tower. There must always be ways to *connect* and create a vibrant, relatable program. Employees need your support and constructive guidance.

None of us walk around thinking we're inaccessible, so how can we know if we are? You might use phrases like, "That's not my job," "I don't have time for that," and "You don't understand," often accompanied by actions like keeping your office door closed more than it's open and only allowing access to you through an assistant.

Remember, compliance is a support function to the business. Treat your colleagues like the customers they are.

Pro Tip from **Stef**

Just like compliance is a support function to the business, so is communications. Since you're both seeking to enable your organization, hopefully this means you'll find a strong partner in your communications colleagues. If that's not the case, it may help to have a conversation with your communications partner about your shared goals. Once they understand the objectives you have in common, they may be more collaborative and supportive.

Ultimately, your best opportunities and most impactful relationships will come as a result of your relationship-building efforts. Moreover, to build deep and wide relationships, it helps to have an open mind so you can consider many sides of different issues. Don't write off a potential relationship simply because you think you won't get along or because the other person comes from a different background. We can learn the most from those who are different from us, whether in terms of background, personality, career status, or any factor.

Intentionally developing lasting and meaningful relationships is a crucial first step toward taking control of and responsibility for your career. No matter how much relationship building you do, others won't make your career happen, and your compliance program won't be improved solely by the virtue of the values it espouses.

You need to put in the work.

This means taking charge and exerting influence where possible. You can absolutely work on building relationships intentionally and consistently—and, over time, you will reap great benefits. Use the resources on pages 140-143 to focus on fostering fruitful, meaningful relationships across your organization.

WAYS TO BE WELCOMING AND BUILD TRUST

Be true to your word
- Honor your commitments in word and in deed
- Always tell the truth
- Keep your values at the forefront

Communicate clearly
- Define roles and expectations, and anticipate and address questions proactively
- Set clear boundaries about scope and responsibilities
- Ask questions to determine understanding and alignment

Build trust
- Give trust to get trust
- Always assume positive intent in others and give respect
- Be mindful about inclusion and create a forum where all voices are heard
- Be reasonable about your expectations, particularly in the beginning or after a challenge

Make decisions carefully
- Be thoughtful about your commitments; only make ones you are prepared to meet
- Recognize that if it isn't a "Hell yes!" it's probably a "No way!" from a commitment standpoint

Be consistent
- Remain consistent to build a reputation of trust and commitment
- Declare who you are and then regularly demonstrate alignment in your statements and actions

Become welcome at meetings
- Show that you trust others by granting space and autonomy
- Listen actively and avoid distractions
- Give any feedback respectfully
- Be a center of calm

Help (even when you don't have to)
- Demonstrate authentic kindness in your daily interactions
- Show your care and empathy for people

Be humble and admit mistakes
- Recognize others first and limit self-promotion to appropriate venues and times
- Show vulnerability to shore up trust
- Seek input and be self-aware (especially of your own blind spots)

CHAPTER THREE

AUDIENCE DYNAMICS: WINNING OTHERS OVER IN THE MAELSTROM

"If you're trying to persuade people to do something, or buy something, it seems to me you should use their language, the language in which they think."

– David Ogilvy, "The Father of Advertising"

As George Bernard Shaw once said, "England and America are two countries separated by a common language." Even with a common language, because of regional and cultural differences, it will be necessary to clarify communication over time. The same is true within corporations and even within industries.

Communicating persuasively demands more than the use of a common language; knowing your audience is critical. Not only will knowing your audience help you determine what content and messages they care about, but—once you have an idea of what to say—you'll also know the tone, voice, and terminology that's appropriate for your audience.

To reach your audience effectively, you must understand the regional, cultural, and other unique attributes of nuance in their vocabulary. The most impactful messages use the exact words the audience uses to describe their own problems.

That's why knowing your audience is so important. Armed with understanding of your audience, all you need to do is get them to tell you about their problems in their own words.

LAUNCH: LEARNING A NEW "LANGUAGE"

Linguists know that learning a new language takes time and exposure. The same can be said for learning a new subject. If you approach learning the "language" of a group, function, business, or company similarly to how you learn a new language, you are likely to succeed.

To that end, consider the LAUNCH acronym:

L — Listen: The most emotionally intelligent and culturally savvy people know that the art of listening is key to rapid understanding. Spending more time listening than speaking allows you to hear unfiltered perspectives and navigate the target language. Go out and hear what people are working on.

A — Ask: Asking good questions advances conversation and comprehension. Connect with people who easily navigate the space you want to influence. Ask about what they are doing with an intent to truly grasp their work and their unique skills, motivations, and perspectives. This is not a time to talk about you, what you are doing, or what you need from them.

U — Understand: As you listen and ask, you can begin to pull the pieces together to understand roles and responsibilities, internal and external motivators, and how your worlds connect to and benefit from each other. Understanding is a continuous process; it never really ends.

N — Navigate/Manage Change: By starting from a place of listening, inquiring, and seeking to understand, you move readily into organizational change management through influence and persuasion. When your audience feels heard and understood, you have done much of the hard work of building trust and credibility—both of which are paramount for the audience's acceptance of new ideas.

C — Communicate: This entire book is about the process of communicating and how important it is to take the whole ecosystem into account. Communication isn't a monologue; it's a collaborative process that requires constant minding and adjustment. To facilitate ongoing collaboration and partnership in moving a common agenda forward, you must stay in touch with your audience both formally and informally.

H — Human Steward Leadership: Steward leadership is often talked about as a philosophical bent that involves bringing out the best in leaders and treating an organization as a purpose-rooted, mission-driven calling, not just as a "job." Steward leaders are caretakers, bringing out the best in the world around them rather than focusing on themselves. Bringing human centricity to steward leadership means focusing on the power of the people within and the impact on others outside the organization. Rooting yourself in the organization's values and strategic initiatives is a good starting point for the "why" of the organization. You should also stay grounded in your personal and professional "why" to establish your purpose, mission, and vision. Once you understand your purpose and how it fits within the organization, the next step is leading with empathy and connectedness. Having connected with others, you can help to cultivate a common agenda focused on overall customers/users, rather than a smaller internal agenda. A common cause and common benefit enables a powerful alignment of effort, which leads to success.

5 TACTICS TO MATCH YOUR PHRASING TO THE AUDIENCE'S

Here are our top five tactics for identifying the exact words your audience uses:

1. **Reviews of the company or its products.** For external stakeholders particularly, look to external resources for information.

2. **Facilitated group discussions.** Joining in on team meetings or project meetings can be invaluable. Also, having a designated time to connect can be useful, whether formally or informally.

3. **One-on-one interviews.** Set up regular meetings with your most critical stakeholders (especially the ones who are fervent supporters or active opponents—The Champions or The Resistance discussed in Chapter 2.)

4. **Voice of the customer surveys.** As we will detail in Chapter 8, the voice of the customer can yield priceless data.

5. **Full immersion.** There are many ways to achieve full immersion. You can shadow someone who works in the target area, attend conferences aimed at professionals you are trying to work with or industries you are interested in, listen to videos, or engage on social media platforms in an area of interest.

The absolute best compliance messages make people feel like you're reading their minds. You speak in their language and can state their pain points, challenges, goals, and desires clearly. If you can demonstrate you understand their beliefs, values, and attitudes toward the situation, they feel understood. You need to be able to describe their concerns and problems more clearly than they can.

The best compliment is "They are saying the stuff I believe but don't talk about."

When you know your audience, you can pluck the words right out of their mouths and use them to support your program objectives.

MOTIVATIONAL INTERVIEWING

As French philosopher and mathematician Blaise Pascal said, "People are better persuaded by the reasons they themselves discovered than those that come into the minds of others." This is where motivational interviewing comes in.

Motivational interviewing, a practice commonly used by psychologists, can work wonders in the workplace. It is highly useful for connecting a person's actions to their purpose and self-motivation. Oftentimes, compliance professionals are entering highly charged environments where there is a reticence to adopting change. Getting true buy-in requires self-motivation and connectedness to the "why" purpose statement. By using motivational interviewing, a compliance officer can help to drive sustainable behavioral change.

Motivational interviewing requires three key communication skills:

1. **Open-ended questioning**
2. **Hearing**
3. **Summarizing**

Open-ended questions are helpful to elicit the speaker's perspectives, as well as the strengths, worries, challenges, and opportunities associated with any proposed relationship or change. This form of questioning is also crucial in building and strengthening a collaborative relationship. When you ask open-ended questions, you allow the person speaking to find ways to communicate and explain their perceptions.

Examples of open-ended questions:

- What is most important in your career/job at this moment?
- What are your priorities and the things you value?
- What are you rewarded for in your career?
- What do you find most rewarding about your work/life?
- In what ways are you living out the organization's values and your own?
- What are some of the things you wish to move forward in your role?
- When you think about the future, what would you like to be able to say?

- If we were to be successful in our work together, what would that look like?

Open-ended questions often begin with *what* or *how*. Open-ended questions lead to discovery and are more qualitative in nature than closed-ended questions, which seem to suggest an answer and are generally more quantitative in nature.

Hearing what is said is important; even more so is affirming what you hear and commenting on the statements. Repeating what the speaker has stated in your own words encourages others to continue talking. This type of engagement building can defuse unpleasant feelings and lead to greater calm. It is also an opportunity to clarify and allow others to correct if something was misunderstood.

By acknowledging and validating the speaker's thoughts and emotions, the speaker feels heard, and you build rapport with the speaker at the same time.

Examples of how to hear well:

- Affirming statements: *"Sounds like this is really challenging. No wonder you feel overwhelmed."*

- Demonstrating concern. *"How does that make you feel?"*

- Paraphrasing to show understanding. *"If I am understanding correctly, you said…"*

- Using nonverbal cues that show understanding, such as nodding, eye contact, and leaning forward.

- Employing brief verbal affirmations, like *"I see," "I know," "Sure," "Thank you,"* or *"I understand."*

- Repeating the information: *"What I hear you say is…," "So you feel…," "It sounds like you…,"* or *"You're wondering if…"*

Summarizing allows a listener the opportunity to reframe the discussion using the speaker's words. Listening with empathy and summarizing what was just said can be a powerful process that leads to change and advocacy by the listener.

Keys to summarizing:

1. Begin with a statement indicating you are making a summary. For example, *"Let me see if I understand so far..."* or *"Here is what I've heard. Tell me if I've missed anything."*
2. Identify key areas of focus, such as recognition of the problem, concerns, intent to change, or optimism.
3. Identify areas of ambivalence that need to be addressed.
4. Always end with an invitation, such as *"Did I miss anything?" "Are there other points or perspectives to consider?"* or *"Is there anything you want to add or correct?"*
5. Focus first on building rapport and allowing people to feel heard so they will give you the opportunity to be a trusted resource in times of change and uncertainty.

Use the worksheet on page 144 to conduct a motivational interview and secure buy-in from stakeholders around change. Keep in mind that motivational interviewing is useful in getting stakeholders to commit and be engaged—both key drivers in sustaining the change.

Self-Determination Theory

The psychological theory of self-determination explains how and why motivational interviewing works, positing that we are more likely to change if three basic psychological needs are attended to:

1. **Autonomy** in making decisions.
2. A sense of our **competence** to make the change.
3. **Relatedness**, or a sense of being supported by key people around us.

The self-determination theory can also be applied in the workplace. Particularly for compliance and ethics professionals, self-determination is useful in driving cultural change. Most people dislike being told what to do or how to feel. People inherently dislike change being demanded of them, but compliance and ethics professionals can help in choosing a path toward productive change. In so doing, they can take some important cues from psychology to help others identify with and choose the desired outcome.

CHAPTER FOUR

UNDERSTANDING YOUR ORGANIZATION'S COMMUNICATIONS APPROACH

"The two words 'information' and 'communication' are often used interchangeably, but they signify quite different things. Information is giving out; communication is getting through."

— Sydney J. Harris, journalist

Perhaps you've never noticed, but your company typically communicates in some common ways. Just like every company has its own culture, every company has certain ways it tends to communicate—formally and informally, internally and externally. This is true whether or not your organization has an in-house corporate communications team guiding its communication efforts.

We begin to learn the flow of information even as children. It starts early, with family systems. Any time communication is taking place beyond one person to another, the flow of information changes and becomes more complex. Children are often adept at figuring out the fastest way to get to their "yes" (e.g., Nana always gives an extra candy, or asking a certain parent for another story at bedtime will yield better results).

The same applies at school; typically there is one person, or perhaps a handful of people, to whom you can pass on a piece of information and then expect the entire school to be in the know by lunchtime. You can call these people gossips or "data royalty," but they are integral to the informal flow of information.

As we join the working world, we learn that information flows differently in an organization–both directly and indirectly–but we may lack the intuition for complex flows that comes from spending an extended period of time in the system. In order to adjust to different flows, we need to be mindful, ask questions, and observe.

STUDY HOW THE COMPANY CURRENTLY COMMUNICATES

As you begin to consider how compliance can best share its content with others, start paying attention to how messages are delivered to you as an employee, what those messages are, and how they're typically approached in terms of tone and method of delivery.

Formal/Established Communication
Channels

Is there an **intranet**, an internal homepage that houses company news and provides links to key policies? What type of company news and/or information is displayed there? How often does it appear to be updated? Do employees have an opportunity to interact with the content by liking, commenting, or sharing it? If so, how many employees are doing this? Does some content get more interaction than other content?

It's important to note that there are all types of company intranets—some much more sophisticated than others. Some are simply a repository of HR-related links to help people do their jobs, while others are true hubs for employees, providing breaking news and other key announcements. If your organization has an intranet, take the time to really understand what it offers and what capabilities it provides. This will help you consider how best to share compliance-related content in this channel.

How extensively does the company use **email** for official communication? Do you receive recurring emails or newsletters from a central communications mailbox, or on behalf of the CEO or another C-suite executive? What type of information do these messages contain? How timely is that information, and how often do you receive it?

Does your organization hold **all-company meetings or town halls**? What type of information is typically shared there, and by whom? How often are these meetings held? How well attended are they, and what type of feedback do you and your colleagues have about these meetings being a good use of your time?

Does your company post **physical signs** throughout its buildings or **digital notices** via employee desktop applications? Where are these located, and what type of content is typically displayed on them? Based on where they're located, what types of employees will see them most often? As an employee yourself, how effective do you consider signs to be in conveying key information as you go about your day?

Volume and Frequency

How would you describe the amount of communication you receive from the company across all of the available channels? Does it feel like too much, too little, or just right? Does it seem difficult to keep up with as you go through your day and focus on your own priorities? Or do you know that when an email comes in or a town hall is scheduled, you should stop and pay attention because you'll receive critical information you can't get anywhere else? Do you know when to expect communication from the company—for instance, every Friday, or the first day of each month?

Informal Communication

Outside of all of the official channels, how does business truly get done at your company? In some cultures, the impromptu hallway chat between meetings is where decisions get made or executives get filled in on key updates. In other organizations, decisions are intentionally restricted to official meetings only, where they're documented in meeting notes and available for all to see. And almost anywhere, the proverbial water cooler (including the virtual one via Slack, Teams, and other chat functions) remains where you can get a pulse on what employees are actually thinking and feeling about what the company is doing and how they're being treated.

We've all worked in organizations with unspoken ways of getting work done. From "the meeting after the meeting" to catching an executive outside his office door or in the break room, these unofficial ways of communicating and working are natural in most workplaces.

When you're considering how to get the word out about something and how to get feedback on what people really think of what you've communicated, don't forget to use these channels—none of which you'll ever see listed by corporate communications as formal channels.

External Communication

If you anticipate having compliance news that would be of interest outside your organization, note how the company communicates to external stakeholders, such as clients, the media, investors, and more. It may not always be apparent to you as an employee, but you can start to get a sense for the way the company communicates externally by studying the company website and the content it publishes in its social channels.

On the **website**, pay special attention to news releases, thought leadership pieces like white papers and blogs, and what the company chooses to promote front and center on its homepage. Who does the company appear to be speaking to most often? What type of functionality, if any, does it offer on the site (e.g., customer login, end-user support, etc.), and who does it seem tailored to? Peruse the investor relations section of the site if there is one, and note any differences in how the company speaks to investors as compared to other audiences. What types of activities is it highlighting? What trends do you see in content across the site, and what does that tell you about what's most important to the company right now? How does that compare to the messages you're receiving internally? Was what you learned on the external site a surprise, or have you already been hearing these things within the company walls?

Do a similar analysis of the company's **social media** channels. Which channels does it have a presence in, and where is it absent? What type of content does the company share on social media, and how often? What type of engagement does this content receive from users via likes, comments, and shares? What is the tone of the feedback—positive, neutral, or negative? Does the company engage with people trying to provide feedback on social media, or does it ignore them by failing to respond or failing to do so quickly? These dynamics will provide useful clues to you about how progressive your organization is when it comes to communicating. You can use these insights to inform the way you communicate as well.

GET INPUT FROM ACROSS THE COMPANY

When you tune in to how your company is already communicating, you'll become more aware of how you—and other employees—consume this information throughout the course of the workday. This is where your perspective as a "regular employee" is incredibly valuable; these are the exact people you'll be trying to reach with your own messages.

Think about when you're most receptive to messages from the company and when you tend to miss them because you're focused elsewhere. What type of content do you pay the most attention to, and why? How much time do you spend consuming content from the company each day or week?

This is a great opportunity to broaden your perspective by asking your colleagues the same questions and noting the similarities and differences in their responses. Don't just ask co-workers in your own department. Talk to friends who work in other buildings or remotely, those who work in other departments, and those on the front lines if possible—on the manufacturing floor or taking customer calls in a different environment than the one you work in.

People in these roles often don't have steady computer access throughout their day or are tightly managed and measured based on their productivity, making it hard to consume content from the company. In fact, they can be notoriously hard to reach from a communications perspective, but often they're the exact audience we need to communicate to. They hold the company's quality performance in the palm of their hand on the manufacturing line. They build up or erode the company's reputation with every phone call they take in the customer service department. While it's challenging that the most critical audience is the hardest to reach, it can be done.

Talk to your corporate communications team about how they're tackling this challenge. Talk to leaders from those parts of the business to understand the specific norms and ways of communicating "on the ground," such as via a quick daily stand-up meeting. This will provide the insight you need to understand how to best get your message to these hard-to-reach audiences.

Use the checklist on page 146 to help you capture the various communication channels your company uses and the type of information shared in each.

5 Questions to Broaden Your Perspective

1. How did you feel about X?
2. What instantly came to mind when I mentioned the topic?
3. What would happen if...?
4. What is in our control?
5. How do you experience me or my team?

More important than asking the question is REALLY deeply listening without judgment. Be curious. Ask follow-up questions. Be respectful and step outside your comfort zone.

UNDERSTAND HOW YOUR CONTENT BENEFITS OTHERS

You're thinking about how and where your company communicates because compliance has something it wants to say to one or more audiences. While you surely have your own goals for sharing this information, you must also be able to convey why it matters to the audience. You'll get much further much faster with your content if you first can speak to how your compliance news or update benefits the end users who will receive it. This will help when and if you need to engage the corporate communications team (more on that below).

Use the worksheet "Why My Message Matters" on page 148 to help you clarify and articulate why your message matters to those who will receive it.

Communicating Effectively with Various Audiences

Employees

If you're looking to communicate with employees, your content must either inspire them to accomplish the company's mission or help them do their jobs better—more ethically, easier, faster, etc. While there may not always be a credible connection between your news and the company mission, sometimes there is one if you dig a little deeper (see the worksheet on page 150 for help with this).

In other cases, your content is more straightforward: for instance, on how employees can complete a task more effectively or how they need to follow a new process to better manage risk for the organization, ultimately helping them do their jobs better.

Work to truly understand which employees you're trying to reach. Take the time to learn what their daily work lives are like and how to best reach them. Remember, you'll need to communicate differently to a technician who works out of a service truck than a corporate employee who uses a computer all day.

Pro Tip from **Stef**

Sometimes you need to communicate to the entire company, but often you don't. Throughout my communications career, I've had this conversation countless times. Someone with something to communicate wants that message to go out to all employees. They're not really sure why; they just know what they have to say is important, and they want to share it as broadly as possible.

In that situation, my job is to help them take a step back and really dig into exactly who needs to know the information and exactly what they need to do with it. During that process, it usually becomes clear that the message at hand doesn't need to be shared with all employees. It's rare that something coming out of one particular department does. That said, I typically appease the desire for broad distribution by restricting an email or direct message to only affected audiences, but offering to post the message in channels that other audiences are consuming more passively, such as in the appropriate place on the intranet.

And yes, this has happened at times in my partnership with compliance departments! For example, you may want the entire company to know about Compliance Week and why it's so important, but from an employee perspective, there's no true timing hook for why they need that information at that moment. They're busy doing their jobs and meeting their deadlines, and unless what you have to say directly affects them, they're likely to tune out. That's why I always counsel my compliance partners to get specific about the exact employees who need to know something, then only communicate to them at the time they need the information.

Clients

If your goal is to communicate with the company's clients, your content should inform them of something they didn't know before or ask them to take a specific action that will help them. Routine, informational updates should be included in a broader vehicle—for example, delivered verbally through an account manager as opposed to through formal communication. Carefully consider whether your update is truly necessary or adds value for a client before sending.

The Media

If you want to communicate with the media, your content must be new or otherwise timely, and it should include your company's unique perspective on the topic. A new product or service is obviously novel and would include the company's perspective, because it's about something the company owns. In contrast, a timely news idea about how companies can be more compliant with gifting around the holidays is not a topic your company owns, so it's critical that your organization's unique perspective on that issue is clear if you plan to share on the topic.

Regardless of the audience, be respectful of people's time. Understand that your audience doesn't have extra time or attention to give to you or your content. They have busy jobs and lives—and a smartphone with much more enticing content than yours to reach for when they have a spare moment. This respect extends to employees, whom companies have historically assumed will tune in just because they collect a paycheck from the institution trying to communicate to them. Savvy corporate communicators now understand they need to compete for employees' attention just like any other audience, and they're acting accordingly. Ensure your content is clear, concise, and directly conveys what the audience needs to know and how it benefits them.

LEARN HOW TO PARTNER WITH CORPORATE COMMUNICATIONS

If your company has a corporate communications team, work hard to build a solid working relationship with these professionals. They're the gatekeepers between your content and the people you want to consume it, and they can help your message be seen and heard much better than you could on your own.

Characteristics of Positive Relationships

Solid working relationships are built on

Trust, Diversity, Mindfulness, Empathy, Authenticity, and Mutual Respect

In practice, the best relationships I have experienced were highly collaborative and cohesive. When I worked with Stef, she brought amazing skills to the table, and her approach allowed us each to be stronger. The "two brains is better than one" adage was so true. Together, we amplified and enhanced the work product. When you get to that level of comfort, you know that the relationship is built to last and benefits everyone.

– Lisa Beth

If your company has a corporate communications team, ask colleagues in your department who they've typically worked with from communications. In larger organizations, you may have an assigned communications contact for all things legal and compliance. If that's the case, ask your colleagues about how they've partnered with that person in the past:

- *What type of support has been provided and on what kinds of projects or topics?*
- *How often is the communicator willing to engage with your team?*
- *What is the process for getting content approved and distributed?*
- *Who determines which channels are best for communicating?*

Many compliance departments won't have an assigned communications contact or may not have partnered with corporate communications before. In those cases, reach out to the leader of the corporate communications team—often a vice president or director-level employee. If your company has an employee directory that displays hierarchy, you should be able to easily identify who this is. If not, ask around or reach out to someone on the communications team for guidance on the best contact. Ask for time to meet with that person about how to best share compliance-related information going forward.

You should also know that many communicators look at themselves as journalists first and foremost. Journalists are storytellers looking to provide an independent view, delivering the right story for the right audiences within their sphere of influence. While it may seem like communication is simply relaying information, true communication is about trying to make an impact with the audience. Always keep in mind the communications team's talent in connecting and having an impact; it's something we can learn from and honor as we treat them like the experts they are.

7 STEPS TO BUILD YOUR RELATIONSHIP WITH THE COMMUNICATIONS TEAM

1. Share how your compliance update benefits the audience you're trying to reach.

When you're clear about this, you'll be speaking the communicator's language and helping them do their job, making them more likely to want to help you do yours. (Don't think compliance content can be interesting or inspiring? See Chapter 5 for how to use the principles of storytelling to make your messages personal and memorable.)

2. Ask about the corporate communications team's goals and how compliance can support them.

This will likely generate similar conversations about how to best serve your audience (for instance, inspiring employees around the company's mission or helping them do their jobs better). However, it may also reveal other goals for communications that will impact your efforts (for example, if your corporate communications team is making a concerted effort to reduce internal email, you'll need to propose other ways to communicate your compliance updates).

3. Show you've done your communications homework.

Demonstrate that you've done your research on communication channels and ask the communicator about the criteria for getting information published in each and about how each channel performs. This is also your chance to learn about any content themes for the next few months that compliance could fit into (often based on an "editorial calendar" the communications team creates), as well as lead times for publishing in each channel and the approval process from a communications perspective. And don't forget to consider these timelines alongside your own department's approval process. Ultimately, to make the relationship work best, you should know your goals for communication and also how your priorities can help communications reach their goals in the process. Always keep in mind the action you want your audience to take and help communications understand those perspectives as part of how the information is presented.

4. Ask for data.

More important than anecdotal feedback is data on the effectiveness of your communications. Check with the communications team about the availability of this data. They will have metrics on which intranet articles are most read, what content on the intranet is most often consumed, and more. They may also have data for internal and external emails that show how many people opened a message, how many "converted" or clicked various links within an email, and more.

Understand what data exists, how often it is monitored and analyzed, and how the communications team adjusts their efforts as a result. Does your content need to meet any minimum thresholds of performance to be considered worthwhile and to open the door to additional communication opportunities in the future? Will you have access to data on how your content performed so you can dig into what worked and what didn't, or does the communications team hold that close to the vest? What should you consider to be a success based on counsel from your communications partner? Be sure to define those goals upfront with their help so you know how successful you were.

5. Clarify the ongoing support you'll receive.

In some organizations, you may be assigned someone who'll partner with you to create an annual communications plan. They may even write all of your communications and help distribute them. In other companies, the corporate communications team may serve as an editor for compliance-related communications, creating plans and writing content only on behalf of executives.

6. Know the processes.

Learn and understand the process for submitting content to a particular channel, which may differ from the approval process. Understand the (often additional) reviews and approvals required for any external communications, like a news release or posting something to the company website.

7. Stay in touch.

Make a plan for how you'll stay connected to the communications department now that you've developed a relationship with them and established an understanding about future support.

While most communicators like me have a greater affinity for words than numbers, I'm here to tell you: data really is a communicator's best friend.

After taking ownership of various newsletters and publications, I've used data to decide to retire them, as the numbers indicated no one was consuming that content. Data has also allowed me to redirect limited resources to create new channels and new types of content and to continually adjust those based on what the readership data told me about their value to the end user.

Data is another method of gathering feedback about what's important to your audience. Use it to the fullest extent.

– Stef

HOW TO COMMUNICATE IN THE ABSENCE OF COMMUNICATIONS SUPPORT

In smaller organizations, there may not be a communications team to support you. Even when that's the case, there will still be approved channels and people to go through to share information, both internally and externally. Someone will be designated to approve these things—perhaps your own department within legal, investor or industry relations, or even the CEO. And, instead of a communicator publishing, it may be an executive assistant, marketing team member, human resources consultant, or someone else. Start asking around—or reply to one of the next company messages you receive and see who responds. Look at who is listed as the media contact on the news releases published on your company website, and reach out to that person. It may take you a few stops to get there, but if you stick with it, you'll find the people who can help you.

The most important thing to remember about communicating without a corporate communications department is to never communicate externally without the express approval of the organization. Know who within the organization gives the requisite approval, and document the approval you receive before sharing anything.

By taking the steps upfront to learn about how your organization communicates and having early discussions with the stakeholders involved, you'll have a strong advantage when it comes time to start communicating about your compliance program and how it will create positive ripples across the organization.

Reference the worksheets on pages 146-153 as you assess your organization's communications approach, plan for conversations about the essential messages you need to share, and develop a pitch to the communications team.

Communications at Startups and SMBs: A Double-Edged Sword

Startups and small businesses have so many advantages in terms of being nimble and adaptable, but with the agility small businesses enjoy also comes the responsibility and added challenge of having to do it all. While trying to draft communications and disseminate information may not have been what you thought you were signing up for in leading a small business, the freedom of communicating easily can be used to help you convey information quickly within your organization.

CHAPTER FIVE

THE STORYTELLER'S SECRETS

"Stories are memory aids, instruction manuals, and moral compasses."

– Aleks Krotoski, journalist and social psychologist

Since the beginning of recorded history, stories have elucidated, changed the way we think about the world, and passed information down through multiple generations. Early humans told stories through music, paintings in caves, and spoken tradition to convey meaning and unite in purpose. Later, stories were conveyed through the written word; great works such as the Ten Commandments, the Vedas, the Bhagavad Gita, and the Egyptian Book of the Dead all gave instructions on expectations of life and codes of conduct.

Pro Tip from **Lisa Beth**

Stories are important to every aspect of our lives. One of the most impactful stories you can tell is the one that conveys who you are and why you are important to the listener. We often call these "elevator pitches" (termed such because they should last no longer than a short elevator ride), which are brief, persuasive speeches used to spark the listener's interest in you, your organization, an idea, etc.

A good elevator pitch hooks the listener in less than fifteen seconds. Have an elevator speech memorized to quickly communicate who you are and what you are trying to accomplish.

WHY DO STORIES HAVE SUCH AN IMPORTANT ROLE IN CONVEYING INFORMATION?

Part of the answer lies in neuroscience: **Stories activate different parts of the brain.** While data-driven information lights up two areas largely focused on language processing, stories light up another five areas (those associated with smell, emotion, hearing, sight, and memories). Neuropsychologist Donald Hebb coined the phrase "Neurons that fire together, wire together," a popular mantra among neuroscientists that means pathways in the brain are formed and reinforced through repetition.

Hearing a story triggers multiple areas of the brain, causing all those neurons to fire together, which helps you remember and retell the story later.

We are wired for story. Storytelling has remained popular for thousands of years because it is a survival mechanism; stories allow us to learn from the experiences of others without directly having to experience the event ourselves.

Stories make us care. The most powerful way to make someone care isn't by telling them what to feel, think, or do, but by telling a story that resonates with them. Creating great communication is like making any meal; if you don't get the ingredients right, it doesn't matter how well you have done on plating and presentation, it's not going to satisfy.

Stories engage our emotions. A good story has the power to make us laugh, rage with anger, fall in love, or cry—sometimes all of these things. This is the most powerful component of storytelling: Stories can compel us to change our behavior by engaging our emotions. Often, we know what we should do, but don't actually do it until we *feel* that we should.

Stories make the abstract concrete. Resistance to desirable behavior often stems from being uncertain of how to act next and failing to understand the incremental impact over time. Someone might know they should eat healthy or exercise, but that advice is too abstract to be helpful. A story of how one person managed their day while eating a healthy diet would be much more helpful in producing change. Stories make the abstract concrete by putting in context how the information will be used and why it is important. Context creates clarity, which eliminates barriers to action.

Making the Abstract Concrete

I once worked with a CEO who was an expert at this skill. He wanted the company to be known for a particular quality, to be unforgettable and so unique that consumers couldn't live without us. But what does that actually look like in real life? How could we aspire to make that happen?

He continually told the story of McDonald's being known for how special their Diet Coke tastes. Who would have thought? I don't know all the details, but apparently McDonald's invests a lot of resources into ensuring their Diet Coke dispenses better than any other fast food restaurant's does, and they've become known for it. People who wouldn't typically be McDonald's customers seek the brand out because of their Diet Coke. It's been years since I worked with that CEO, but this story stays with me because it helped make the abstract concrete.

–Stef

Stories help clarify what we should do. They provide specific examples of what to do and what not to do in situations. Truly, a story is a way for us to perform mental simulations and analyze different options without having to go through the actual experience. In the business world, this would be helpful in crisis response simulations; the learner can understand what they should do in several situations without having to live through a variety of actual emergencies (thankfully).

Stories teach us cause and effect. It can be easy to lose sight of your position and the larger consequences of each action.

Through storytelling, the learner can come to understand the full effect of their actions on others. For instance, stories of people making what seemed like logical decisions that led to negative consequences can be very powerful in providing guidance in decision making.

A good example of stories teaching us cause and effect are contained in the context of perverse incentives. An incentive is intended to motivate and reward a person for engaging in certain behaviors or driving certain outcomes, but it becomes perverse when there are unintended (and often undesirable) results.

The "cobra effect," named by economist Horst Siebert, occurs when an incentive designed to solve a problem actually makes the problem worse. During the British rule of India, officials in Delhi became increasingly concerned about the number of wild cobras in the city. To reduce the population, the government established a bounty on cobra skins. Soon, dead cobras were flooding the local government. However, at the same time, some budding entrepreneurs decided to raise cobras to be sold for the bounty. The government soon caught on to the entrepreneurial endeavors and terminated the bounty program. However, the story didn't end there. The cobra-raising entrepreneurs, left with worthless live cobras in their care, decided simply to release the cobras, further increasing the population of wild cobras within the city.

Perverse incentives have dire consequences in compliance as well. There are plenty of examples of sales incentives leading to undesirable behavior, and many bribery and corruption stories begin with incentives for sales growth that were taken too far. Perhaps the most well-known recent example of a perverse incentive is Wells Fargo: When salespeople's jobs and bonuses were on the line and tied to account growth, fake and unauthorized accounts proliferated.

THE NEUROSCIENCE BEHIND EFFECTIVE STORYTELLING

Stories give us a common point of reference and help us to relate to each other. They allow us to share a moment of common history while also increasing our empathy and reinforcing pro-social behaviors like kindness, compassion, and philanthropy. But there's also a scientific reason stories make an impression the way they do.

From a biological perspective, stories compel us in three ways:

- They help us bond through emotional experiences.
- They force the left and right side of the brain to connect more deeply.
- They afford us "practice" and mental muscle memory in a safe environment.

The Love Hormone Facilitates Strong Bonds

What's love got to do with it? Oxytocin (also known as the "love hormone") is the chemical released by the brain when we connect with people we care for, like children and other loved ones. Through storytelling, we can experience simulated bonding, as if we were meeting a friend, even though we don't have any real relationship with them.

Wiring Your Left and Right Brain Together

Language, communication, facts, and data activate two parts of the left side of our brain. The left side of the brain is rational, focused on data and analytics, and tends to work well with concrete concepts and patterns. The right side is often considered the more creative and colorful part of the brain, where abstract concepts and big-picture themes go to live. The right side of the brain is also where intuition and gut instincts reside.[2]

Stories bring together both sides of the brain in beautiful harmony. The language and information target the data and analytics side of the brain, while the big picture and themes of the story arc stimulate the right side of the brain. When we hear a story, both sides of the brain operate simultaneously, combining memory functions and experience functions with data.

The power of emotion and story—often over facts!—was best summed up for me recently by a colleague when he asked which statement is more impactful:

- You can reduce disease transmission 95% by wearing a mask.
- Don't kill grandma.

Because of the way our brains are wired to feel the story, a few words are more meaningful and more likely to drive a change in behavior than all the numbers you can find.

– Lisa Beth

---

[2] Cohut, Maria, Ph.D. "How language shapes our brains ... and our lives." *Medical News Today*, February 22, 2019. https://www.medicalnewstoday.com/articles/324529

Mirror Neurons Help to Form Strong Emotional Memories, Safely

A mirror neuron is a neuron that is activated both when a person is in action or experiencing an emotion and also when a person sees the same action or emotion performed by someone else. Essentially, mirror neurons allow a person to have a simulated experience by observing someone else. [3]

These neurons often cause us to subconsciously mirror the actions or emotions of others, which explains why we cry in sad movies and why our hearts race during a thriller. When we watch someone drowning on film, we feel the need to hold our own breath, and we may experience the fear and anxiety as if we were the ones stuck in the sinking ship. Our mirror neurons help us connect with these experiences so that we literally express the physical manifestations of a movie character's actions and emotions.

Our emotions are a signal to remember an experience. When we feel emotions, the attention and memory-making areas of the brain are triggered, letting our brains know that the information is important. The more deeply we feel the emotions, the more deeply these memories are stored in our brains. When we connect on an emotional level with a narrative, we are much more likely to be able to remember key parts of and retell (or "relive") the story.

---

[3] Bastiaansen, J.A.C.J.; Thioux, M.; and Keysers, C., "Evidence for mirror systems in emotions." *Philosophical Transactions of the Royal Society of London. Series B, Biological Sciences.* The Royal Society, August 27, 2009. https://www.ncbi.nlm.nih.gov/pmc/articles/PMC2865077/

NEURAL COUPLING
A story activates parts in the brain that allows the listener to turn the story in to their own ideas and experience thanks to a process called neural coupling.

DOPAMINE
The brain releases dopamine into the system when it experiences an emotionally charged event, making it easier to remember and with greater accuracy.

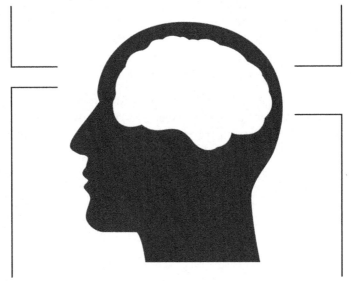

MIRRORING
Listeners will experience similar brain activity not only to each other, but also to the speaker.

CORTEX ACTIVITY
When processing facts, two areas of the brain are activated (Broca's and Wernicke's area). A well-told story can engage many additional areas, including the motor cortex, sensory cortex, and frontal cortex.

3 TIPS FOR CRAFTING AN EFFECTIVE STORY

If you want your story—personal or professional—to have a greater impact on others, keep these things in mind:

1. Capture Attention Through Conflict or Tension

Attention is the brain's most precious resource. For the brain to expend its energy on taking in new data, there must be something at stake. A story that creates tension is likely to capture our attention, as our brains see the possibility of learning something that could help us avoid a threat or take advantage of an opportunity.

In marketing, there is often a fine line between causing unnecessary stress and bringing attention to a problem that a product or service could help resolve. In storytelling, it is the relatability of the character's problem to our own that makes our ears perk up and draws us in.

Tension and conflict have been used throughout time to generate listeners' interest. Both promote the anticipation of release or resolution. Common methods of incorporating tension and conflict include time pressure, drama, plot twists, withheld information, and cliffhangers.

2. Put Yourself in Their Shoes

To build empathy and a sense of connection, think about how your audience will be able to relate to your story. What are their greatest desires and fears?

Cater your story to the people you want to help or entertain the most. Think about the stories you are drawn to. They are likely ones you can most easily see yourself in.

Present your story so your target audience gets to be the hero—you just happen to be the "guide" who helps them navigate through a problem, sort of like a personal Yoda.

If you are successful with these first two strategies, you will help your audience experience a phenomenon called "transportation." Through transportation, we enter the "land" of the story, thanks to a cocktail of cortisol (from our heightened attention) and oxytocin (from our sense of shared connection).

We can all agree that the issue of human trafficking is sobering and overwhelming in its magnitude, but it can be easy to tune the problem out because we think in numbers, not in terms of individual people.

If you were to communicate about human trafficking with your employees, you might share details about your organization's policy pertaining to modern slavery, as well as what the organization expects of them. That's what most compliance professionals would do. Alternatively, you could tell them a story that helps them put themselves in the shoes of a victim of human trafficking. Suddenly those numbers aren't just numbers anymore—they're about a real person.

Consider the example of Kaitlyn, a young girl who was angry with her parents for being too strict at home. Sick of all the boundaries and expectations at home, Kaitlyn decided to run away with her best friend, Amanda. The two best friends left and went to a truck stop, looking for a ride to Florida, where they planned to live at the beach. It was a bit colder than the girls expected, and they ended up seeking food and shelter from the wrong person. So began their descent into the world of human sex trafficking. After their first encounter, the girls were too ashamed to go home, convinced their families would never accept them again. And so the cycle of abuse and slavery continued not far from their hometown.

Everyone can imagine a Kaitlyn or Amanda. In reading the story above, you may even have pictured a Kaitlyn or Amanda who you've known personally. Details like these help your reader step into the shoes of the impacted parties. Which would you be most likely to remember down the road when you actually needed to apply this information—details about the company's human trafficking policy, or the story of Kaitlyn and Amanda?

3. Use Time-Tested Techniques to Propose a Solution in a Novel Way

Building your stories using time-tested techniques that are common throughout recorded history can allow your audience—regardless of their differences, including geographic location, life experience, cultural background, etc.—to internalize the controlling idea and test it using newly found ethical and compliance muscles, or retest what they already know.

The underlying elements of all stories are nearly identical (character types, setting, plot, conflict, theme). What differentiates a story is the novelty of the content or the way the content is structured. The element of novelty means that you are able to create a new experience by making a slight change. In retelling a familiar story—even with the same basic characters—you can achieve dramatically different results and even send a different message. Consider the numerous adaptations of *Cinderella* or *The Secret Garden*; Disney is a master of this art.

Novelty increases information recall. To help your audience remember or act on your message, present it in a new and unique fashion. Because the brain has to pay more attention to retain new information, it is more likely to remember data presented in a novel manner rather than in clichés.

Some of our favorite movies, television shows, and books can help us to connect with storytelling truths we have experienced. As you consider the stories that captivate your attention, you will begin to see themes you relate to.

Starting conversations around scenarios from popular movies or TV shows can spark powerful engagement about ethical dilemmas. For example, the Harry Potter series gives many memorable examples that can be explored to discuss topics such as theft, class bias, an "ends justify the means" mentality, and so on.

TYPES OF STORIES

To understand stories and how to shape them, it's important to know some of the mechanics of good storytelling. The narrative arc, or the "story arc," is a reference to the structure and shape of a story. The arc incorporates all the events in the story (although the sequence of those events is called the plot), and it determines the pace, peaks, and plateaus. No matter the form your story takes—written, visual, or auditory—the arc moves the audience from beginning to end and delivers a satisfying conclusion.

According to research done by the University of Vermont and the University of Adelaide, there are six primary classical arcs based on what happens to the protagonist, or hero. In their research, they used artificial intelligence to collect computer-generated story arcs for nearly 2,000 works of fiction, and the results were subsequently featured in an article in *The Atlantic*.[4]

Because of the universal nature of these story arcs, they are called archetypes and follow a common pattern, even though there is mild variation. The six core types of story arcs (and examples) are:

1. **Rags to Riches** [a complete rise]
   (*Annie, Aladdin*)

2. **Riches to Rags** [a fall]
   (*The Picture of Dorian Gray*, early seasons of *Schitt's Creek*)

3. **Man in a Hole** [fall, then rise]
   (*A Christmas Carol, The Hobbit*)

4. **Icarus** [rise, then fall]
   (*The Hunger Games, The Great Gatsby*)

5. **Cinderella** [rise, then fall, then rise]
   (*The Little Princess, Jane Eyre*)

6. **Oedipus** [fall, then rise, then fall]
   (*Gone with the Wind, Flowers for Algernon*)

Compliance and the Moral of Morality Stories

Most of the compliance and ethics stories we tell are short and aimed at instilling the value of the targeted action. We try to give our audience the opportunity to simulate a real situation, with the very low stakes of it being a story. Because the stories typically involve ethical or rules-based dilemmas, the subplot of a morality story often comes into play.

---

[4] LaFrance, Adrienne. "The Six Main Arcs in Storytelling, as Identified by an A.I." *The Atlantic*, July 12, 2006. https://www.theatlantic.com/technology/archive/2016/07/the-six-main-arcs-in-storytelling-identified-by-a-computer/490733/

A typical morality story involves a single protagonist whose inner moral compass actively changes (or actively refuses to change) along a spectrum that runs from selfishness to altruism. Morality stories teach us how to make critical decisions and evaluate consequences. They teach us about proper behavior within the expectations of our environment, how to show greater leadership, and how to make good choices in alignment with commonly held values. Morality stories may act as the catalyst to change and help to enforce the values or ethos of the community to which we belong. These stories remind us of the expectations of behavior, give an opportunity to practice in a safe environment, and educate us about the consequences.

Morality stories typically have a controlling idea or theme: the lesson each listener or reader will understand at the end of the story. Controlling ideas help to connect the theme with the sought-after emotions. Emotions typically seen in morality stories include pride, happiness, sadness, surprise, fear, pity, contempt, and other similar emotions. At the end of many morality stories, audiences experience the satisfaction of seeing the protagonist receive a proper outcome.

WHAT IF I DON'T HAVE MY OWN STORIES?

Not everyone has an arsenal of compliance stories they can tell from a first-person perspective or that they have previously identified. If you don't have your own stories or stories that would make sense within your company, look to stories within your industry or country that might make sense.

In the compliance context, here are some examples of the six types of stories:

Rags to Riches
[a complete rise] (Ben & Jerry's)

The classic rags-to-riches story is embodied in the story of two ice cream makers extraordinaire, Ben Cohen and Jerry Greenfield. Starting from humble beginnings, their first venture, a bagel business, failed. But out of that failure, the friends launched Ben & Jerry's. Due to the anosmia (inability to smell) of one of the founders, the ice cream makers decided to use larger chunks in their recipes, and a worldwide craze was born.[5]

At the center of Ben & Jerry's success was a commitment to doing right while doing well. They have remained true to their values and commitments despite acquisition by a large corporation, and the company's avid following makes this a wonderful rags-to-riches story rooted in values.

Riches to Rags
[a fall] (Kenneth Lay at Enron)

In the late '90s and first few years of the 2000s, Enron was all the rage. Everyone was talking about the smartest men in the room and how they had revolutionized the energy and utility industry. While some questioned how they were making all of this money legally, many others focused on the results rather than the "how."

Kenneth Lay was the CEO of Enron. At one point in time, he was one of the highest-paid CEOs in America. He was paid millions upon millions in cash and sold off more than 1 million shares of stock.

As the problems with Enron multiplied, the former leader of the most "innovative" energy company found himself without a job,

---

[5] Fabry, Merrill. "Ben & Jerry's Is Turning 40. Here's How They Captured a Trend That Changed American Ice Cream." *Time*, May 4, 2018. https://time.com/5252406/ben-jerry-ice-cream-40/

and at the time of conviction, he apparently had a net worth of -$250,000. He died of a massive heart attack before sentencing.[6] This is a fairly classic riches-to-rags story that cautions against cutting corners and failing to listen to warnings, as well as surrounding yourself with "yes" men.

Man in a Hole
[fall, then rise] (Sex trafficking)

Modern slavery and any form of human trafficking is a blight upon society. While we talk about the problems associated with human trafficking, we cannot do so in the abstract. The most impactful stories about real compliance issues put faces on real-world consequences.

> While I worked at Carlson Wagonlit, a travel management company, the philanthropic work the company did with rescued trafficked people seemed most impactful when communicated through the stories of people who had been sold into trafficking, who had run away, who had been manipulated, and who were plucked from vulnerable populations. Their stories are important to tell, and the work being done to create paths to better lives is profoundly important.
>
> **– Lisa Beth**

Icarus
[rise, then fall] (Elizabeth Holmes at Theranos)

Stories about the perils of a rise without appropriate governance and the inevitable fall can be very impactful.

---

[6] Teather, David. "Kenneth Lay." *The Guardian*, July 5, 2006.
https://www.theguardian.com/business/2006/jul/05/corporatefraud.enron

The story of Elizabeth Holmes and Theranos is just such a story, with its shockingly unblinking CEO who styled herself after Steve Jobs and surrounded herself with a vanity board of directors all while the technology was nonexistent. The writings of John Carreyrou in the media and his book *Bad Blood* set the stage for the unicorn-level rise and then the terrible fall of Theranos.[7]

Cinderella
[rise, then fall, then rise] (Martha Stewart)

Stories about a fall and then a rise can be used to motivate people into action both to prevent and to improve conditions.

Martha Stewart began life as the second of six children in New Jersey. She was a teen model turned homemaking maven. Her empire and image of domestic perfection was reaching millions of American households regularly. From deals with Sears and a widely circulated magazine to television appearances, everything seemed to be coming up Martha.

That is, until December 2001, when she allegedly received a tip to sell ImClone stock to avoid losses. While the government never was able to convict her of insider trading, she was convicted of felony conspiracy, obstruction of justice, and lying to federal agents, a conviction that landed her in prison and under house arrest with probation.

After her return to work, Martha worked to rehabilitate her brand and her primary occupation. Her estimated net worth in 2020 was $400 million—not the $1 billion estimate in 2000 prior to the insider-trading prosecution, but also a respectable rise after a devastating fall.[8]

---

[7] Carreyrou, John. *Bad Blood: Secrets and Lies in a Silicon Valley Startup* (Knopf, 2018).
[8] Hays, Constance L. "Prosecuting Martha Stewart: The Overview; Martha Stewart Indicted by U.S. On Obstruction." *The New York Times*, June 5, 2003. https://www.nytimes.com/2003/06/05/business/prosecuting-martha-stewart-overview-martha-stewart-indicted-us-obstruction.html

Oedipus
[fall, then rise, then fall] (Lance Armstrong)

Lance Armstrong represents a great example of a fall, then rise, then fall, much like Oedipus.

For many years, Lance was a professional bicycle racer, most famous for his work in bringing American interest and viewers to the Tour de France. However, in 1996, he was diagnosed with a potentially lethal metastatic testicular cancer. He was treated and went into remission.

Lance began cycling again and managed to win seven consecutive Tour de France titles as well as a bronze medal in the 2000 Summer Olympics.

Allegations of doping began in 1999 but were originally fended off quite easily. It was not until 2012 that the U.S. Anti-Doping Agency concluded that Armstrong was the ringleader of "the most sophisticated, professionalised and successful doping program that sport has ever seen."[9]

* * *

The universal appeal of a good story is a great way to connect with any audience. It's your job to find the right story for your audience and to capitalize on the brain's wiring to make a connection and help your message stick. In this way, you'll illustrate the audience's role in the success of the compliance program and how they'll benefit, gaining not only their compliance, but also their interest.

It's critical to make it clear to your audience how to take action and apply the lessons from the story to change their behavior.

---

[9] Cohen, Kelly. "The rise and fall of Lance Armstrong: What you need to know before watching 'LANCE.'" *ESPN*, May 21, 2020. https://www.espn.com/olympics/story/_/id/29177242/the-rise-fall-lance-armstrong-need-know-watching-lance

Because stories are often associated with entertainment or our childhoods, we don't want people to mistake them as simply interesting; we're using them for a reason: to make our information more memorable and to inspire people to take action.

So, tell great stories, but don't forget to be explicit about the action you want people to take as well.

Complete the worksheet on page 154 to begin developing your storytelling narrative.

CHAPTER SIX

RIGHT MESSAGE, RIGHT AUDIENCE, RIGHT TIME

"Nothing in life is more important than the ability to communicate effectively."

– President Gerald R. Ford

You've probably heard the saying, "Timing is everything." It's a favorite among communicators because it's profoundly true. A message your audience completely ignores one day can easily become the center of their attention the next based on what's going on around them.

While we can't always plan for or control all the factors that contribute to catching someone's attention, there is a lot we can do to get the right message to the right audience at the right time. It all starts with **understanding what your audience cares about and how your information benefits them**: how your content fits into their world—what they want, what they need, and how you can help improve their jobs or lives in some way.

From there, determine **the timing for communicating with your audience based on their needs**. They'll be most receptive to your message if they receive it right before they actually need it. This "just in time" delivery helps them process your information and quickly take the needed action in response. Take, for example, communication around holiday gifting policies; your audience will be much more receptive to this message in late November than they will be in August.

While that may seem obvious, other examples will be less clear, and compliance departments have been known to let their own priorities drive the timing of communication. However, it's important to always think from the end user's viewpoint and deliver the information when it will be most relevant and timely for them.

Speaking of the compliance department, what happens when your priorities don't align with the needs of your audience? For example, your boss wants to get a message out on her timing, but she isn't considering all the other content hitting employees that week. Or a client-facing communication is written with a focus on benefits to the company, not to the client. In these situations, you must balance the audience's needs with compliance's goals, with a bias toward audience needs.

While this can feel uncomfortable at times, it will make your message more effective in the end. If your department publishes something it's happy with but that only serves your goals, you might temporarily feel good about getting it done, but you'll be unhappy later when no one reads it or takes the action you need them to take. Use the worksheets on pages 156-159 to help you plan for and reconcile disparities in the needs of the compliance department and the audiences you're seeking to reach.

Pro Tip from **Stef**

What's the best way to keep an audience-first mindset when creating compliance communications? It's to constantly monitor what employees actually care about.

Take a step back as an employee yourself. What's on your mind? What challenges or opportunities are you facing, and how could compliance partner with you to address them?

For those in companies with robust intranet sites, another great approach is monitoring likes and comments on intranet articles. The big topics, like company earnings, rarely get much employee engagement, but announcements about news that directly impacts employees—such as pay, benefits, or changes to work arrangements or spaces—will garner significant engagement. Take note of what content employees interact with and the sentiment of their comments, and think about how you can use that insight to inform the communications you plan to do on a given topic.

5 KEY PUBLICATIONS MILESTONES

Once you determine how to get the right message to the right audience at the right time, you need to work backward from your ideal delivery or publication date to set milestones to accomplish all the necessary steps that need to happen beforehand. This will vary greatly by company but can include any of the following:

1. Approvals

How many rounds of approvals are required for the content? Who provides the ultimate sign-off? This may apply both on the compliance side and within communications or any other group involved in this content based on the topic.

2. Translations

In multinational or global companies, it's often required, even legally, to translate key information into local languages. Depending on your company culture and the specific information you're communicating, you may need to plan time for translations and understand the process for getting content translated.

3. Publication

You'll also need to know required lead times for getting content published in various company channels. Certain vehicles may have schedules, but content may "book out" well in advance on editorial calendars. You'll want to plan for this as you work backward from the ideal timing for your audience to receive your message. Finally, the communications team will likely require a certain number of days to process your content—giving it any final edits, queueing it in systems for publication, and more.

4. Advance notice/pre-inform process

Consider which groups, if any, need to receive an advance copy of your content before you share it with your ultimate audience. Depending on the culture of your organization, this might include executive or leadership teams of the departments involved in creating and producing the content, departments involved in managing relationships with the end-user audience, or others.

5. Printing and/or shipping lead times

Printing and shipping deadlines can add significantly to the lead time required to produce content and get it into the hands of your audience, so plan ahead for this if applicable. (It is becoming less applicable, since increasingly fewer corporate materials are created as physical copies; depending on your situation, however, it could still apply.)

Use the worksheets on page 160-163 to help you identify what applies in your organization and how to manage it all.

Finally, consistently and regularly monitor the feedback your audience is giving you about the content you're sharing with them. In today's social media world, there are more ways than ever to engage in two-way dialogue with your audience, whether that means monitoring the tone and sentiment of comments on articles or webpages or analyzing actual statistics on open rates, clickthroughs, or time spent reading web-based content. Your corporate communications department can help you understand what's available and how you can get access to that information. Use the worksheet on page 164 to help you keep track of audience feedback and generate your own ideas about other ways to listen to your audience.

Compliance and ethics can oftentimes be frustrating. Links and connections that you see may not be ripe or seen by others yet. Early on in my career, I experienced a situation with environmental, social, and governance (ESG) reporting. It was the early days of these efforts—a time when it was still called "corporate social responsibility."

As a young securities lawyer, I had a point of view on the importance of repeatable and consistent measures of performance that were created to meet reporting standards. I felt very strongly that over a period of time, ESG would mature and the smaller groups of stakeholders that were requesting visibility, transparency, and accountability would grow larger and likely impact SEC reporting for public companies.

There wasn't much agreement about those perspectives then, but I chose my timing and audience strategically to begin developing support. As part of the work, I spoke the "language" of each audience to win them over. For finance and accounting, I spoke in terms of auditability and reporting. For legal, I spoke in terms of disclosure risk and liability. For the public relations and ESG leaders, I spoke in terms of trust, credibility, responsibility, and the reputational risk of "greenwashing."

It was important to sequence communications, use language that resonated, and center the message on values to win others over. The message was timed properly to begin the journey—although my ideas about the importance of ESG and reporting took a little longer to rise to the prominence we see today.

— **Lisa Beth**

Pro Tip from **Stef**

Learn from this communicator's mistakes! Don't just plan time for translations; plan time after you receive the translation back to have a native speaker within your company perform a quality check. Even high-quality translation services require a check from local language speakers to capture local dialects and other nuances that can be hard to capture from a central resource. It's always wise to check it internally.

If your company doesn't have an established roster of people around the world who will help with this, here's your chance to put in place something that will benefit the compliance department and others company-wide!

CHAPTER SEVEN

SAY IT AGAIN: REPETITION MATTERS

"Repeating is the whole of living, and by repeating comes understanding, and understanding is to some the most important part of living."

— Gertrude Stein, author and poet

The common wisdom is that people need to hear something seven times before they remember. This is so true. Corporate communicators understand the power of varied repetition to break through the noise and reach audiences with their messages. Compliance professionals must do the same so their content is received.

In fact, it's never been more important to repeat your message. We all walk around with tiny computers in our pockets that ping us with constant news updates, messages from friends and family, and advertisements trying to get our attention. Recent estimates indicate that most of us hear up to 30,000 words each day and receive up to 10,000 marketing messages trying to sell us something. It's no wonder information overload is at an all-time high, resulting in distraction, trouble concentrating, and difficulty remembering important information.

We all understand this on a personal level, but we may not think of applying this knowledge in terms of how we communicate with others. Don't assume your message was received by your audience just because you communicated it one way, in one channel—it's very likely that it was missed by most. That's why many communicators use the phrase "seven times, seven ways" to describe the varied repetition required for their messages to break through.

Repetition from the Consumer's Point of View

How many times have you realized immediately after a coupon has expired or some promotional event has ended that you needed whatever that thing was? You weren't paying attention to those messages until you had a need for the information. Then, when the topic does become relevant, you suddenly notice all the commercials or billboards related to that topic in your daily life.

For example, your car breaks down and, unexpectedly finding yourself in the market for a new one, you notice for the first time how many car dealership commercials run during the evening news. This is why varied repetition is so important: People are busy, and they might not be receptive to your message quite yet. Continue to serve up your content in different ways at different times, and you'll increase your likelihood of breaking through the noise.

A logical question many compliance professionals may ask next is, "Why create even more noise by repeating my message? Am I just contributing to the chaos?"

Yes: If you're not intentional about how you repeat your message—being mindful that it adds value each time—you will contribute to the noise. That's why the key point here is to communicate using *varied* repetition, meaning you focus on different angles and employ different formats to share the same core message over time. In other words, this isn't a copy-and-paste exercise in which you continually share the same message over and over.

Variety is the spice of life; the adage is also true when we are talking about communication. Given the diversity of the modern workforce, we need to be able to communicate in many different ways for our message to resonate with multiple audiences. Some learners are very visual, others learn more effectively by hearing, and still others retain information better through active learning involving motion.

What we know about *all* learners is that repetition matters. That's why it takes a few times to hear a new advertising jingle, a new song, or a new quote to be able to sing along or repeat the message.

> Some retain a message best if they can be creative in their own ways with it. One of the most powerful ethics campaigns I've seen involved regional competitions for publicizing the core messages of Ethics Day. Sharing the approaches of multiple offices all over the world led to great learning moments and memories to last a lifetime.
>
> – **Lisa Beth**

LEARNING STYLES: DIFFERENT PEOPLE LEARN DIFFERENTLY

Before we discuss the different ways you can create varied repetition in your communications, let's consider another way variation will be valuable to your audience (beyond simply breaking through the clutter and getting noticed in the first place). People also absorb and retain information in different ways, making it critical that you vary how you communicate to be as inclusive as possible.

Depending on which source you consult, researchers have identified anywhere from four to eight learning styles that impact how each of us filter and process information in our worlds. The four most common learning styles are:

1. Visual/Spatial

These people learn by seeing pictures, charts, or video footage. They require some type of visual aid to process and remember information. Communications that include diagrams, photos, infographics, or video clips will be most easily remembered by visual/spatial learners. Because communicators seek to distill complex topics into visuals that can be quickly digested by audiences, often on tiny screens, current communications trends tend to favor visual/spatial learners. Infographics and videos are more widely used now than ever before, as people of all learning abilities seem to have less appetite for long articles that require a lot of scrolling on their screens.

2. Auditory

This group learns by hearing information and often verbally repeating it in their own words. They rely on the spoken word to filter and retain content. Communications that occur in a live setting, like town halls or small group meetings, are best suited to auditory learners because they can not only hear presenters give information, but also interact by asking questions and repeating what they've heard to confirm understanding. Another great option for communicating to auditory learners is via podcasts, where they can listen to what the speakers are saying and reflect individually on the content.

3. Kinesthetic/Tactile

These individuals learn by experiencing or doing—think about museums where visitors can interact with artifacts, or learning about birds in the course of a nature walk rather than by reading about them in a book. This type of learner is typically harder to accommodate with traditional corporate communications approaches, but there may be small ways to consider kinesthetic/tactile learners with your content.

When this group can interact directly with content, such as choosing which information they'd like to consume in which order, they'll remember it best. So, you could serve up your content in small "chunks" with varied formats on an internet landing page, allowing kinesthetic learners to "choose their own journey" in terms of how they want to navigate through the page and consume the information. You can also integrate videos and other formats that are more likely to make the viewer feel as though they're participating directly in the experience.

4. Reading/Writing

These people learn by consuming written words, usually by reading or by writing—or rewriting—the information themselves. While there can be some overlap with visual learners, given that reading/writing learners are viewing words, the difference is that they retain words much better than they do pictures or other visuals.

Traditional corporate communications cater well to reading/writing learners, as they tend to center around the written word. But, as previously mentioned, there's less appetite in general for long, written communications these days. To bring these learners along as you lean more heavily on shorter, more visual communications, include closed captioning on video and captions under photos so they can still read along. These elements also help people with disabilities better consume your content. (Consult your corporate communications department for more specific guidance on how to make your communications more inclusive to people with disabilities. They'll likely have guidelines by channel.)

These learning styles are why I believe well-produced, company-wide internal meetings are such effective communication vehicles: They deliver something for every learning style, all in one venue. There are slides and other visuals through which attendees can consume data. Attendees hear presenters verbally sharing the information. And they often get a bit of an experience, like watching a panel discussion or seeing a video.

If your company offers a meeting like this throughout the year and your content is relevant enough to be included, congrats! You've struck gold in terms of getting your information absorbed by those with different learning styles.

— **Stef**

HOW TO VARY YOUR MESSAGE

Beyond accommodating the various learning styles, your message will have a better chance of breaking through the noise and being remembered if you focus on different angles and formats to share the same core content.

To vary messaging with your specific piece of content, you'll start by identifying the core concepts associated with your message. These are the "who, what, why" details that are fundamental to the subject you're trying to communicate and, therefore, won't change as you vary your delivery.

It's critical to start by outlining these core details to identify what won't vary in your messaging, even as you change other elements. If these details aren't consistent across your communications, you will confuse your audience. For example, if you're not clear on the "when" aspect of your message and you communicate contradictory date and time details across different messages, you're creating discrepancies that will confound your audience and erode your message's effectiveness.

What's my role?

Audiences consume information passively or actively. When they listen passively, they are less engaged, less likely to retain information. Passive listeners don't recognize there is something they need to do imminently with the message being transmitted. Generic messages are often consumed passively.

Active listeners, on the other hand, generally understand that they have a role, that something must be done, and that it is their responsibility to do it. As a result, they focus on more of the details.

Bearing passive versus active communication in mind, consider the role or roles of your audience to help them engage more deeply in the communication. As you communicate with your intended audience, you must help them become active listeners by conveying that they need to take action. Clearly communicate who your information pertains to, why it matters to them, and what they need to do.

Once you've identified the core details in your message that won't change, you'll start to brainstorm how you can vary the message by audience and channel. Complete the worksheet on page 166 to identify those aspects of your message that will stay the same, regardless of the audience.

Variation by Audience

Think about when your information will impact the audience and what you want them to know and do after consuming the content. This may look different for different groups of people affected by your message, so complete the exercise in the worksheet on page 167 for each audience you're trying to reach.

Once you've reflected on all of this, consider whether any of these elements could create a new angle for sharing your content.

For example, let's consider the "when" element of the core details surrounding a company's holiday gifting policy. The finance department might be impacted in early November because they need to start monitoring purchasing for any noncompliant requests. The average employee, however, doesn't need to be informed until after Thanksgiving in the United States, when they're more likely to start thinking about the holidays. Using this information, you can create two varied messages, each focusing on the unique timing hook for when each group will be impacted by holiday gifting.

Later, you could reach each audience again with the same core information on holiday gifting by focusing on the "how" element of the core details. Your instructions for how finance can help enforce the policy will differ from the details other employees need on how to abide by the policy. In this way, you're continuing to communicate about the policy using varied repetition, focusing on different angles of the same core message based on what each group needs to know.

Variation by Channel

Another way to create varied repetition is by using different channels to communicate your information, reinforcing the importance of the work you did in Chapter 4 to understand your company's communication vehicles. The beauty of varied channels is that they will by nature force your message to be different (for example, consider the amount and type of content you can communicate in an intranet article compared to a social media post with strict character limitations).

What might this look like in real life?

Revisit with us the holiday gifting policy.

- As an employee walks into the building, a teaser about the policy could be displayed in hard copy on an easel near the elevators.
- When they log in at their desk and open their internet browser, they could see an intranet article explaining the policy in detail.
- Then, throughout the months of November and December, as they enter conference rooms, a reminder about the policy could be scrolling on digital screens.
- The policy could also be reinforced on table tents throughout the cafeteria seating area.

While this particular topic likely doesn't merit this kind of attention, this is an example of how you can deliver the same message in different ways via different formats to stay in front of your employees on critical issues.

For each of the channels available, consider any character or other length limitations. Then consider whether each channel can support different formats—pictures, audio, video, graphics, and more. Based on that, think about how you can deliver your core content differently across channels to create varied repetition and appeal to different types of learners, as outlined above.

For example, you can plan to reach employees about the holiday gift policy by creating an intranet article that goes into greater detail about the policy and the actions you want employees to take, including an infographic about the five steps to follow the policy.

You may also reach employees using a short visual on digital screens throughout the office building, pointing people to the intranet article for more details. Finally, you can put a short, 140-character "teaser" about the gifting policy in the company's internal social media channel, again linking to the longer intranet article for more details.

Use the worksheet on page 168 to plan how to vary your message according to the particulars of each channel and format.

As you set out to create varied repetition, remember the "seven times, seven ways" rule. The average person must hear something seven times to remember it—so repetition isn't optional, it's a necessity. But great communicators go beyond basic repetition to serve the same core content up in multiple ways. In the process, they create communications that are more audience-focused and more interesting to consume, making them more memorable in the first place. It's a virtuous cycle, and one that any compliance professional can skillfully do with some forethought and planning. Ultimately, messages and communications are measured at the listener's ear—the legacy of your message is what is impactful and memorable for the listener.

Use the worksheets on pages 167-169 to help you think through all the potential variations for your particular message. Also, refer to the guidance in Chapter 4 on how to partner with corporate communications to create content that they'll support disseminating to your key audiences.

CHAPTER EIGHT

THE LISTENING ADVANTAGE: THE GIFT OF FEEDBACK

"No communication takes place until the other person feels heard."

– Garrison Wynn, author and motivational speaker

The act of distributing or publishing a message is just the beginning when it comes to communicating with your intended audience. Most people who aren't communication professionals don't realize this. Instead, they assume that once their content has been disseminated, their job is done. Actually, this is when the real process of communicating begins!

While this hasn't always been the case, it's truer than ever today. Why? Because in this age of social media, almost every message can be liked, shared, and commented on. This is even true for internal communication, as companies increasingly enable social sharing functionality on intranet articles and embrace internal social media channels like Yammer or Slack.

FEEDBACK IS A GIFT OF TIME AND ENERGY

It isn't easy to be honest with people—especially in a corporate setting and when the message isn't necessarily positive. If someone has taken the time to give feedback, it is both a duty and an honor to listen to see how your work can be improved and better meet the needs of our audience.

All of this is great news from a communications standpoint, because—unlike in the past, when messages were sent out into the void with little to no response—we now receive insight into whether people understand our message, agree or disagree with it, or have questions about it. We can use that insight to provide additional information to achieve our ultimate goals of sharing important information and ensuring it resonates. Plus, the dialogue between the company and one employee can be seen by others, benefiting all.

However, this level of transparency also creates risks. Objections and challenges are now available for all to see, rather than being limited to a single phone call or email, as in the past. The way the company—or in this case, the compliance department—responds to those objections will be on full display as well. Compliance professionals need to plan ahead for how they'll handle any negative feedback in a public forum. Negative feedback is most likely to come during a crisis response, when you won't have time to plan in advance how to handle it. That's why it's so important to make those plans ahead of time, during normal operating mode.

Another change is the fact that people expect real-time dialogue when having conversations on social channels. It's no longer acceptable to spend several days crafting the perfect response in formal, corporate language. When people take the time to engage with your content and share their questions or feedback, they expect quick acknowledgement and an authentic reply.

4 WAYS TO MITIGATE RISKS AND MAXIMIZE OPPORTUNITIES ASSOCIATED WITH 2-WAY DIALOGUE

1. Assign a Point Person

You should determine who on the compliance team will take the lead to respond to feedback or questions resulting from your communication. This person should be the one most well-versed in the topic at hand and, therefore, the one best able to quickly provide clarification as needed. Given this, the point person will likely change from message to message, based on who has the most knowledge of a given topic.

For those who are a department of one, the responsibility sits squarely on your shoulders. When you are a department of one, it is important to be crystal clear on your scope and priorities. Balancing multiple duties—for monitoring, reporting, planning for potential challenges, and so on—can feel overwhelming and a bit daunting to handle by yourself. It is important to remember that building relationships, as we have discussed in prior chapters, can include support from other departments and individuals. You are never completely alone on this journey.

2. Regularly Monitor

Decide as a team how often the point person should check for feedback on the published content to promptly respond to any submitted questions or comments. Ideally, this would be once in the morning, once midday, and once before the workday ends for about a week after your content is published.

You'll be watching for any potentially negative or sensitive responses you need to quickly address (see below) and engage with those sharing positive feedback. Thank them for their support and for taking the time to engage with you.

3. Plan for Challenging Responses

In most cases, the point person should be empowered to respond to any feedback about the communication. In rare cases, a comment or question may be sensitive and require additional oversight before a response is provided. This could include content that is inappropriate, in which case the commenter is likely in violation of a code of conduct pertaining to the company website or social channels (employees are likely subject to additional company policies regarding social media use and conduct). In other cases, the comment may be particularly negative or may include personal information that's best shared privately—each of which require a careful response. In still other situations, the topic itself may be sensitive enough to merit extra scrutiny for any response.

As a compliance team, it's critical to anticipate the types of challenging responses that could arise from a given topic and determine how each situation will be handled, including the escalation and approval chain. Once again, even in challenging situations, a timely, authentic response is expected from those who engage with you. And from the company's perspective, these are the types of responses you want and need to quickly address. So make plans now for how to be nimble and responsive when needed.

4. Look for Trends

As you receive questions or comments about the content you've communicated, keep an eye out for commonalities in the topics that arise. If five or more people ask the same question or express the same concern, it likely means your communication should have proactively addressed this topic. Depending on the situation, it may be appropriate to update the original communication, to issue a revised message that clarifies additional points, or to create and share a frequently asked questions (FAQ) document that addresses these items.

Alternatively, you may receive an overwhelmingly positive response to your content, such as when you've updated a long-outdated policy to make it more relevant and applicable to employees. Pay attention to this feedback, too, and think about how you can apply it to other parts of your work. For instance, using the policy update example, you may decide to prioritize updating other outdated policies that affect employees, because it's clear this work is meaningful to them and creates goodwill and credibility for the compliance department.

With a proactive plan in place for mitigating risks and maximizing opportunities, compliance should proceed with confidence and seek to communicate as often as possible through channels that enable transparent, two-way dialogue.

Finally, don't forget about the more traditional methods for gathering feedback, like via an email to the compliance inbox, written notes left in a comments box (yes, some companies still have these!), or a good old-fashioned phone call from someone who wants to share their thoughts. While the feedback in these cases won't be visible to the entire company, it should still be compiled with the comments you receive elsewhere and considered when looking for trends or monitoring stakeholder sentiment in response to your message. Use the worksheets on pages 170 – 173 to track audience feedback and plan your responses accordingly.

THE NUMBERS DON'T LIE

Even when employees aren't engaging in two-way dialogue, you can gather feedback on the effectiveness of your communication using the metrics available from various channels.

For external audiences, this includes:

- Time spent consuming your content on company websites;
- Likes, comments, shares, and reposts on social media; and
- Third-party publication of your messages via news outlets or blogs.

For internal audiences, metrics include:

- Time spent consuming your content on intranets;

- Likes, comments, shares, and reshares in internal social media; and

- Open rates and clickthrough data for internal emails.

To be able to interpret these metrics as feedback, you need to benchmark the performance of your communication against that of other content published in the same channels. By partnering with your corporate communications department, you can receive information about the average performance of other content, then understand how your communication compares. Is it about average, or in the top or bottom quadrant in terms of performance? This provides an indication of whether your intended audience was interested in what you had to say, which you can use to inform future efforts.

That said, don't forget to take into account unrelated factors that could have had an influence on the performance of your communication. For example, if you share a message the afternoon before Thanksgiving in the U.S. or during your target audience's biggest deadline of the year, the odds are good that many people missed your communication and it won't perform well, even if your audience values the content. This speaks to the importance of careful planning in advance around timing and partnering with your communications team to avoid these mistakes in the first place.

Don't wait until you're communicating to get familiar with the metrics available to you, though. Corporate communications can likely enroll you to receive a recurring report (often monthly or quarterly) that shows top- and bottom-performing content and the topics associated with each. Take a quick look at this information to understand the content employees are most and least interested in. Look for trends or other clues that could be applied to compliance messages to help them perform better.

For example, you might notice the top content each month is often a poll question that hundreds of employees respond to. How could you integrate a poll question into your content, or use one to preview a topic you plan to communicate about shortly after? Even better: You could use the insight you receive from poll responses to shape the content you create and the information you share!

SEEK OUT THE VOICE OF THE CUSTOMER

Pro Tip from **Lisa Beth**

Directly asking how others are feeling is always a great first option, but people seldom like to give face-to-face feedback, particularly if it is less than positive.

One way to deal with this hesitation to provide candid feedback is to offer an anonymous feedback mechanism. For the same reason that it is helpful to have a way to report concerns anonymously, it is also helpful to give your key stakeholders an opportunity to serve up anonymous feedback.

A voice of the customer program is a common way to collect feedback, and it's a technique you can use in your compliance program as well. It captures, analyzes, and reports on all feedback—expectations, likes, and dislikes—associated with your program. When done properly, seeking this type of feedback will give you insight into your audience's experiences. And from this feedback, you can identify trends and opportunities to improve the reception of and buy-in on your program and gain critical momentum for any changes.

There are many reasons to consider a voice of the customer approach, including that it gives you insight into potential problems and barriers before these issues become intractable. Compliance professionals should expect friction at times, but anticipating and addressing pain points before they fester allows you to operate smoothly and be more effective.

3 Key Areas of Focus When Implementing Voice of the Customer

1. Consistency. Everyone starts at a baseline. You need to regularly engage with the same people and ask the same questions to determine whether whatever you're measuring (e.g., the audience's perception of the compliance department, their understanding of certain policies, etc.) is improving for those impacted by your program.

2. Multiple Voices. You need a critical mass of the members of different groups and a consistent methodology for identifying them. Seek input from across the organization, in many functions and at multiple levels.

3. Storytelling. The results from your audience should be woven together to tell a story. Asking for candid input and including some open-ended questions the audience can use to provide anecdotal feedback makes a difference. Using the words of people who have experienced the compliance program is a powerful way to tell the story of the impact and effectiveness of compliance in your organization.

A voice of the customer program must do all of the following:

- *Provide oversight.* Elicit and track insights through a design and oversight process.

- *Listen.* Pay attention to what the feedback in all areas tells you.

- *Communicate.* Feedback shouldn't go into a black hole; there should be a feedback loop that lets people know they have been heard and that there is action taking place.

- *Analyze the root cause.* Transform the information you receive to identify key trends and insights on potential improvements.

- *Take action/remediate.* Once you identify challenges and barriers, establish a game plan to correct the problems.

- *Audit/monitor.* Track your progress over time. Progress isn't always linear, and you may not be able to eliminate a challenge within a year, but it is important to demonstrate momentum and changes you've made over time.

Ask the Right Questions

There are many questions you can ask to elicit feedback on your compliance program. They need to be tailored to your organization, but the following are a good starting point. (You can also access these questions on the worksheet on page 174.)

What support are you looking for from the compliance program?

This question is often a great way to start. It allows you to understand the expectations the audience has to begin with. This question removes inhibitions and directs attention to the audience's needs or wants. When you ask this type of question, you set the tone that the compliance program is part of the company team and that you care about the perceptions of the compliance program.

Just as we all have different experiences in our lives, your audience may have wildly diverse expectations. As the survey recipients respond, pay close attention to the words they use. Even if responses are similar, the language and context can give you additional clues about how the program is being perceived.

What words would you use to describe the compliance program?

This question provides you with words to be used for storytelling and gives you a deeper sense of the immediate reaction of the survey recipient. It gives you insight into their current feelings about the program. While their feelings may change over time, it gives you a good window into the current state of how the compliance program is perceived.

In what areas does compliance really excel? In what areas can the compliance program improve?

It's important to understand what your audience already thinks compliance does well; those are areas that should stay the same or not change much. The areas for improvement may be ones that have caused the most pain points for your stakeholders. Not everyone is going to like compliance, but they shouldn't unnecessarily dislike the program. You may find you have opportunities to more clearly communicate and to clarify misunderstandings to strengthen your relationships.

What's your biggest complaint about compliance?

You need to understand how the audience sees compliance—both the good and the bad. You may gain critical insights into lags in responsiveness, communication gaps, or any of a host of addressable issues. You may also discover unrealistic expectations that need to be clarified for a common understanding of both the capabilities and limitations of compliance within the organization.

What should compliance keep/stop/start doing?

This gives you real insights into the challenges, opportunities, and triumphs of the compliance program.

Keep: This is the list of things that are already going well. You want these efforts to maintain momentum over time, because they are already effective. The answer to this question identifies triumphs and can serve as part of the compliance program's highlight reel at the end of the year.

Stop: This is the part of the survey that can identify counterproductive practices and gaps that make the team lose credibility and momentum. Often, a "stop" will readily suggest a "start"—an immediately obvious solution.

Start: This is the section that points to key opportunities. There may be some areas you didn't realize needed attention or where there's a need for modification. Maybe there are practices other parts of the organization are doing that you could adopt. This section will likely be more difficult to read, as it presents opportunities that may be couched as problems.

GATHERING VOICE OF THE CUSTOMER FEEDBACK

Now that we know what we want to ask, how do we go about soliciting feedback?

Consider providing your target audience with a series of short surveys. (If you're able to conduct shorter surveys more often throughout the year, you may end up with more participation and greater insight.) Having a "pulse" survey approach can provide you with real-time data that's more accurate and useful in the moment.

In addition to the questions outlined above, ask for an "overall" rating. This forces your audience to rate their feelings quantitatively, instead of relying on qualitative or anecdotal feedback, which can be hard to take action on. Strategic use of yes/no questions can also generate information that's easier to analyze. Even so, ask both qualitative *and* quantitative questions, because anecdotal feedback can be useful—particularly in storytelling, as we've discussed.

It's critical to respect respondents' time by keeping surveys relatively brief, but it's also important to get to the question behind the question: the "why," which forms the root cause of your challenges. This type of feedback is exceedingly helpful as you look at program reforms.

There's a science to creating statistically sound surveys that avoid leading questions, refrain from combining topics that prevent analysis on either one, and more. Larger organizations often have internal survey teams you can work with to review your survey content. In fact, depending on the size of the group you're planning to survey, you may be required to work through them to administer the survey through the company-approved tool and on timing that considers other surveys happening at the same time. In smaller organizations without that resource, you could ask a reputable third party to review the survey before it is disseminated.

CONCLUSION

While you've reached the end, we hope it's not the last time you read this book. In fact, we've designed it to serve as a manual for both current and future communications about your compliance program—one you can revisit for a refresher or a gut check throughout your career. To that end, we hope it won't be long before the corners are tattered, the pages dog-eared, and the margins marked up with smudged ink—all the makings of a trusted guidebook, which is what we've sought to create here.

We hope that any time you need to gain buy-in and share information to promote change or improvements within your organization, you'll find new value in both our words and the resources we've provided. One thing we know from doing this work is that it isn't always easy. Our work together has involved delivering hard messages to people who often don't want to hear them. If you do this work long enough, you'll find yourself there, too. Remember, when it comes to communicating, clear is kind. Think about your audience first, share what they need to know when they need to know it, and know that the rest will sort itself out.

Furthermore, we hope you'll use the tenets we've shared here—such as focusing on your audience and their needs—with colleagues outside of compliance and even personally. As we all know, communication is the key to success in any relationship. (Perhaps you won't be surprised to know we've used some of these tools and tricks with our spouses, to great effect!)

By applying what you've learned here, you'll do more than earn your place at the table when it comes to decision-making; you'll position yourself as a valuable, respected resource from whom leaders seek input before the decisions need to be made. We wish you every success on your journey to become an organizational scholar, an integral member of your organization's leadership team, and an effective, engaging communicator.

Please communicate with *us* by letting us know how you've used the content in this book, what questions you have as you work through it, and anything else that's on your mind. We'd love nothing more than to have a conversation with you and use your feedback to refine how we approach this topic in future endeavors. You can reach either of us on LinkedIn anytime.

ACKNOWLEDGMENTS

Thanks from Stef

I would be remiss if I didn't start by thanking Lisa Beth! You've been a beloved colleague, mentor, and friend to me for the past decade, and the respect you've earned in the compliance industry is what has given us the opportunity to share this book with the world. Thank you for trusting me to bring this message forward alongside you, and for the countless other doors you've opened for me throughout my career. I'm so grateful to you!

Thank you to the amazing communicators I've gotten to work for and with over the past fifteen years. This profession has given me the best network and friends anyone could ask for. Thanks especially to Shannon Coughlin for taking a chance and hiring me as a recent college graduate all those years ago, then patiently teaching me everything I didn't realize I desperately needed to learn. She gave me audacious opportunities I didn't deserve at that age, taught me how to influence without authority, and cared about me deeply as a person, not just a worker. Shannon and so many other communicators have done more for me than I could ever repay.

Thank you to my beautiful family: to my husband, Troy, for always doing whatever it takes to enable me to focus on getting my work done—including all the extra things I take on (this book included!)—and for always caring about what I have to say; and to my kids, Logan and Claire, for giving me a reason to model what a great work life can look like, even if I've gotten it wrong more than right over the years. I hope each of you will also receive the gift of discovering what lights you up at a young age and figuring out how to get paid to do it as an adult. I promise it's not just hard work, but a ton of fun.

Finally, thank you so much to the team at CCI Press for believing in this idea enough to make it the second-ever book you've published! Sarah, Sam, and Emily, you are absolute pros. I'm so grateful for your careful stewarding of these ideas into something that will best serve the compliance industry.

Thanks from Lisa Beth

First things first, to my dear friend Stef, thank you for your friendship, smarts, guidance, and support in all things life, career, and as part of the adventure of writing this book together. From the moment I met you, I knew that you were exceptional in your field and as a business leader. You bring out the best in everyone you meet, and I am so grateful to have been a recipient of your advice, expertise, and friendship in the process. Thank you for sharing your amazing talent with me (and the world) and for being my partner in this work we brought to life. (We did it!)

Along the way, I have been so incredibly lucky to be surrounded by leaders who care. I cannot possibly list all of the wonderful influences I have had (that would be another book). That said, I am eternally grateful for the leaders who have taken the time to invest in me throughout my career. I am also thankful for the coworkers who have inspired me along the way.

The SEC gave me an entire community of Staffers to connect with based on our common mission of integrity in financial markets.

Best Buy was a family of Blue Shirts who brought the art of possibility into the world by connecting people and taught me critical lessons in values to: unleash the power of our people; learn from challenge and change; show respect, humility, and integrity; and have fun while being the *best*.

CWT's mission to connect the world through travel gave me the opportunity of a lifetime with genuine, amazing people who I cherish as valued friends to this day.

Deluxe taught me the importance of agility.

And at Lumen, I get the best of all worlds by being able to use my voice on my own terms to help others put their values into action.

A huge thanks goes to my family. My parents taught me persistence and have always believed in me, constantly pushing me to be the best version of myself and not to accept "less than." To my brother, without whom I would have been an only child… Seriously, Nate, you make me proud every day and force me to chillax at times. My Type A personality benefits from your counsel when I get way too uptight or lose balance. To my aunts, uncles, and cousins, thank you for being part of my village and for always being that support I need, in both the good times and not-so-excellent times. Thank you to my husband, Kevin, for knowing me as a friend since I was a 1L and for seeing my sparkle even when it had dulled. You lift me up and are my rock. I will always choose you as my leader for the Zombie apocalypse. And a huge thank you to my children, Luke, Lucinda, Liam, and little Lili Marlene. You have been so excited to see mom featured in magazines and now a book. You know that it takes lots of hard work, but that work is not as hard when you love what you do. You are my circus, and I am so happy that I get to be the person you call "Mom." I love you all!

I echo Stef's thank you to CCI Press. It is a rare gift to be able to work with people you think are at the top of their game, and CCI Press is absolutely the premier publishing house for compliance and ethics books. You are incredible professionals and made this dream come alive.

Thanks from Both of Us

We would also like to thank Henry Chessin, Dawn Bryant, Jerry Hogan, Michael Voss, Mat Watson, Susan Anderson, Barbara Boehler, Mary Shirley, and Dan Ayala for their input and candor. As our core team of beta readers, the gift of their time and professional insights was priceless in refining this work. We cannot thank you all enough for your support and feedback.

WORKSHEETS

EVENTS ROADMAP

Use this worksheet to note key events for your organization. These key events can be translated to a company calendar, which will be helpful in your efforts to connect with your organization and become (and remain) a scholar of your organization.

Holidays (Statutory and Otherwise)
....
....
....
....
....

Annual Surveys/Reports
....
....
....
....
....

Conferences
....
....
....
....
....

Quarterly Events
....
....
....
....
....

Annual Events
....
....
....
....
....

Board Meeting Dates
....
....
....
....
....

Worksheets

Investor Calls

....
....
....
....
....

Newsletters

....
....
....
....
....

Product Launches

....
....
....
....
....

CEO Addresses

....
....
....
....
....

Campaigns

....
....
....
....
....

Town Halls

....
....
....
....
....

UNDERSTANDING YOUR ORGANIZATIONAL BRAND

Use this simple matrix as a starting point to identify how the organizational brand is being used in different contexts. You may find that there are many external groups or multiple brands, depending on the organization. Expand the matrix to incorporate the elements and to identify the differences and similarities.

View	Articulated Values / Value Proposition	Benefits or Core Message	Position
External			
Both Internal and External			
Internal			

Ask yourself:

- What does your organization do? Be concise. Does it differ depending on the audience (customers, community, employees, etc.)?
- Why does your organization do what it does? What's the passion and purpose behind the business?
- What industry or industries is your organization in, and how does it compare to others?
- What makes the organization unique?
- How would you describe your target buyers? Are you selling business to business (B2B), business to consumer (B2C), or a combination?
- What is the language used to describe the organization internally, externally, and in other locations? Does it differ? Can you determine why?
- What words would you use to describe your business? What "personality" is associated with the organization?

INITIAL INTERVIEW ABOUT COMPLIANCE AT THE ORGANIZATION

Use this worksheet in your preliminary efforts to get a read on the perception and efficacy of the compliance function.

Can you provide me a bit of background about the history of the compliance function at the organization?

....
....
....
....

What current problems need to be solved?

....
....
....
....

How did we get here?

....
....
....
....

What are we doing today that is not working?
....
....
....
....

What opportunities are we missing? In what areas can we improve?
....
....
....
....

Do you foresee any specific future problems for the program?
....
....
....
....

If you were the compliance officer for a day, what would you continue to do? What would you stop doing immediately? What would you start doing ASAP? Why?
....
....
....
....

How can we work together better?
....
....
....
....

PERSONAL STAKEHOLDER MAP

Use this worksheet to assess each stakeholder's level of commitment and determine the actions needed to enhance agreement and trust.

- List all key stakeholders for your compliance program.
- Identify the last meaningful contact you had with the stakeholder (e.g., group meeting, 1:1, etc.).
- Place an "X" in the column that denotes their **current** stakeholder type.
- Place a "☺" in the column to denote the **desired** stakeholder type.
- Describe the desired state and what that would look like.
- Plan your next step and approach to moving from the current state to something closer to the desired state.

Worksheets

Stakeholder Name	Last Contact	Neutral	Challenger	The Resistance	Champion	The Resilience	Desired State
Bob	3/1, 4/21	Next Steps & Approaches: *Identify Bob's critical deliverables and find ways compliance can make his life easier.*			☺		Champion
		Next Steps & Approaches:					
		Next Steps & Approaches:					
		Next Steps & Approaches:					
		Next Steps & Approaches:					
		Next Steps & Approaches:					
		Next Steps & Approaches:					

ENGAGING WITH YOUR STAKEHOLDERS

Use this worksheet to begin developing relationships with your stakeholders, including planning interactions to build and maintain collaborative partnerships company-wide.

Prepare Through Research

If you don't know the stakeholder, spend about fifteen minutes researching the person in question.

This should not be exhaustive research, but rather a simple process using publicly available information. Search their name on Google, then peruse sites such as:

- Facebook, Twitter, Pinterest, YouTube, or Instagram to see what they are interested in and what is important to them.
- LinkedIn to better understand their professional background and any other affiliations they may have (e.g., alma mater, philanthropy, etc.).
- Any other public blogs.
- Any internal corporate announcements, news, or resources.

It's good to update this process from time to time. If you have administrative or team support, you can delegate some of this activity as needed. It's important that you have a system to keep information about key stakeholders current and vibrant.

Find Something Unique to Be Curious About

When you are reviewing materials, take note of unusual activity on social media or elsewhere. Is your stakeholder a superfan of anything? Do they regularly use hashtags when posting?

One way to connect is to be curious about something they appear to like. For example, the stakeholder may be liking posts about Malta. If so, why not ask if there is any special connection they have to Malta?

Typically, if you hit the mark with your research, you will get someone to talk about what they are truly interested in and passionate about. By asking questions and listening intently, you can lay a strong foundation for an ongoing relationship.

Seek Information That Isn't Too Personal as Conversation Starters

If you can't find anything truly unique, sometimes you can find easy ways to connect based on geography, prior career experiences, or education. Key things to consider:

- What companies have they worked for previously?
- What do they seem most proud of?
- Where have they lived geographically?

With information like the above, you can use conversation starters such as:

- "I noticed that you have a connection to a women's leadership organization. What inspired you to join that group?"
- "I saw that you went to college in Appleton, Wisconsin. My grandparents live there. Have you ever supported businesses on College Avenue?"
- "Before you went to law school, it looks like you spent time working in an art museum. What was that like?"

Always be careful not to be too adamant about the information you have. It's one thing to be curious (although potentially incorrect); it's another to appear creepy.

Use Common Ground to Connect on a Deeper Level

People crave connectedness. Having some sort of common ground seems familiar and safe. So, when you can, finding shared interests is a great way to support a relationship.

It's great when you can connect quickly and deeply. However, any good connection will form the basis for an improved relationship. Consider how you could connect on interests such as hobbies, travel, literature, entertainment, LinkedIn networks, social causes, or philanthropy.

Develop Your Stakeholder Profile

This example is one that has worked for me:

Name	Function	Family	Groups	Food & Drink	Interests	Other
Lisa Beth	CEO	4 children, ages 2-15, husband former USMC	ESG, Women in Leadership	Foodie!	Theatre, travel, well-being, art	Law school professor, attorney, polyglot
Stef	Founder	2 children, husband in golf industry	Women in Leadership, PR Comms	Fan of coffee breaks	Storytelling, college essays, yoga	Master's from U of MN

This example can be used in an Excel spreadsheet for your personal use. It can also be used in the "Notes" feature of the contact profile in Outlook. If you have a client relationship management tool, this type of data can be helpful as well in the format available to you. The key is to use tools that work for you to remember key elements of your stakeholders in a way that helps you connect and build strong relationships.

Stay Focused

It's important to build relationships and then continually reconnect to keep those relationships vibrant. However, you have to strike the right balance. If you end up having lengthy discussions on social topics, you may not leave enough time to have the impactful business conversations necessary to establish or maintain your professional presence. Don't let your connectedness be a detractor or an impediment to the business objectives at hand.

We recommend spending the first three minutes of a thirty-minute meeting on social connection, or the first five to six minutes of a sixty-minute meeting. If the personal conversation is still going strong at that point, a great way to transition to business is to say something like, "I'll be sure to schedule lunch with you sometime soon to finish this discussion, because I want to know more than we have time for today." Statements like that indicate you're interested and want to continue the discussion, and they also close the topic so you can transition to the work at hand.

Become Valuable to Others

Focusing on how you can help people will highlight areas where you need to invest in learning, and it will teach you how to calibrate your responses based on their needs. Over time, more and more people will come to you for advice, and you will become a go-to expert. In the process, you'll develop empathy and social awareness to help you read people, relate to them, and become even more valuable.

MOTIVATIONAL INTERVIEWING AND GAINING BUY-IN

Use this worksheet to prepare for a discussion with a team member once change is contemplated.

What are the most important reasons to make this change?

....
....
....
....

What are the benefits to you/your team/the organization?

....
....
....
....

Name some other times you have been successful with a situation like this.

....
....
....
....

In what ways was the prior change successful?

....
....
....
....

What might get in my way?

....
....
....
....

How can others help me?

....
....
....
....

What similar steps and help can I use this time?

....
....
....
....

How will you know that the change is successful?

....
....
....
....

COMMUNICATION CHANNELS CHECKLIST

Use this checklist to help you identify the available communication channels for your company, how they're maintained, and how users engage with the content.

INTERNAL

Channel/ Vehicle	Frequency	User Engagement & Interaction	Notes and Observations
☐ Intranet ☐ Contains news articles	☐ Daily ☐ Weekly ☐ Monthly ☐ Other	☐ Likes ☐ Comments ☐ Shares	☐ ☐ ☐ ☐
☐ All-company town halls	☐ Weekly ☐ Biweekly ☐ Monthly ☐ Quarterly ☐ Biannually ☐ Annually	☐ Attendance ☐ Feedback	☐ ☐ ☐ ☐ ☐ ☐
☐ Company emails	☐ Daily ☐ Weekly ☐ Monthly ☐ Other ☐ Biannually ☐ Annually	☐ Readership (anecdotal feedback from colleagues; actual metrics from corp comms)	☐ ☐ ☐ ☐ ☐ ☐
☐ Signs	☐ How often used? ☐ Location?	☐ Anecdotal feedback	☐ ☐
☐ Other	☐	☐	☐

EXTERNAL

Channel/ Vehicle	Frequency	User Engagement & Interaction	Notes and Observations
☐ Website	☐ Daily ☐ Weekly ☐ Monthly ☐ Other	☐ Likes ☐ Comments ☐ Shares	☐ ☐ ☐ ☐
Social Media Channels ☐ Facebook ☐ Twitter ☐ LinkedIn ☐ Instagram ☐ YouTube ☐ Snapchat ☐ TikTok ☐ Other	☐ Weekly ☐ Biweekly ☐ Monthly ☐ Quarterly ☐ Biannually ☐ Annually	☐ Followers ☐ Likes ☐ Comments ☐ Shares	☐ ☐ ☐ ☐ ☐ ☐ ☐ ☐ ☐

WHY MY MESSAGE MATTERS

Use this worksheet to help you clarify the goal for your communication with each audience, balancing the compliance department's goals with audience needs.

Who is your audience? What do you aim to accomplish with your message? How does your message meet that goal?

Consider this example:

Audience: **Employees**

Goal: Inspire them to accomplish the company mission.

How: Consider the "so that" to connect the goal to the company mission.

> "Employees need to know about this policy change SO THAT they can do their jobs more effectively SO THAT they can eliminate errors SO THAT doctors get the equipment they need SO THAT doctors can do more timely surgeries SO THAT we can accomplish our mission of being the most reliable ambulatory surgery center in Cincinnati."

Whereas you might not have made the connection before, now your communication can say ***"This policy will ultimately help doctors do more timely surgeries, furthering our mission to be the most reliable ambulatory surgery center in Cincinnati."***

When you can help people connect how the small things they do support the broader purpose of the company, you're more likely to get their attention.

Audience: **Employees**

Goal: Inspire them to accomplish the company mission.

How: ....

(or)

Goal: Help them do their jobs better.

How: ....

Audience: **Client**

Goal: Inform them of something new.

How: ....

(or)

Goal: Ask them to take specific action.

How: ....

Audience: **Media**

Goal: Provide new or timely information.

How: ....

(or)

Goal: Share the company's unique perspective.

How: ....

Audience: ....
Goal ....
How: ....

Audience: ....
Goal: ....
How: ....

PREPARING TO MEET WITH CORPORATE COMMUNICATIONS

My topic and why it matters to the audience (use output from the previous worksheet):

....
....
....
....
....

What are your department's goals, and how can I support them?

....
....
....
....
....

My initial observations about company channels and user engagement:

....
....
....
....
....

What's the process for getting content published in a particular channel, like the intranet? (Note: this will be different from the content review and approval process.)

....
....
....
....
....

What measurement data is available on communications? What should I know about it, and what does corporate communications do with it?

....
....
....
....
....

How will compliance and corporate communications stay connected going forward?

....
....
....
....
....

GETTING YOUR MESSAGE OUT

After your introductory meeting with the communications team, you should have a wealth of information you can use to create your first proposal to them for sharing compliance content. Pick a specific topic that will be relevant for employees to learn about two or three months from now and use the worksheet below to craft your pitch to the communications team. Use the example below to help you get started, then fill out the worksheet on the following page with your own topic and how it applies.

Topic: Holiday gift giving and receiving

Requested timing and rationale *(why it is relevant to the audience at the specified time)*: Early November, before teams need to order client gifts and before they start receiving gifts from external vendors.

Goal: Help employees do their jobs better.

How: While holiday gift giving is a great way to show gratitude and appreciation at this time of year, it's important to abide by the company's gifting policy so we don't unintentionally break the law, putting ourselves and our clients at risk. Keep Scrooge out of your holiday gift gifting by following these three guidelines.

Contribution to corporate communication efforts: Will be done in an infographic style, contributing to communications' desire for new content formats beyond standard articles

Requested channel and rationale: Company intranet news section to maximize the likelihood that employees see it

Other relevant notes: Check on copyright issues with referencing Scrooge/including photo in infographic

Recommended approvers: From legal/compliance: Director of Compliance, VP of Compliance, CCO (final)
From corporate communications: Director of Internal Communications (final)

Topic:
....

Requested timing and rationale *(why it is relevant to the audience at the specified time):*
....
....

Goal:
....
....

How:
....
....

Contribution to corporate communication efforts:
....
....

Requested channel and rationale:
....
....

Other relevant notes:
....
....

Recommended approvers: From legal/compliance: _____, _____. and _____ (final)

From corporate communications: _____, _____. and _____ (final)

DEVELOPING YOUR STORYTELLING NARRATIVE

Use this worksheet to build impactful stories that compel your audience to action.

Who is the main character?
....
....
....

Who are the other characters?
....
....
....

What is the hook to make this interesting to the audience?
....
....
....

What does the suggested arc do to help further develop the character(s)?
....
....
....

What is the problem or dilemma?
....
....
....

What is the solution or result?
....
....
....

What is the theme or lesson?
....
....
....

Write the story:

BALANCING STAKEHOLDER NEEDS WITH COMPLIANCE GOALS

Complete this worksheet to establish what your audience wants and needs to understand from your communication, compared with what the compliance department wants and needs to communicate. Identify where those wants and needs align and where they diverge, and plan ahead for how to approach any issues you identify.

Audience Wants/Needs	Compliance Wants/Needs
Audience #1: General Employees	
They care about: Receiving perks and recognition from vendors around the holidays	*We care about:* Enforcing our corporate gifting policy
Why? Everyone loves gifts!	*Why?* It's our job to manage company risk
They need to know: That giving and receiving corporate gifts must be done within very specific parameters	*We want audiences to know:* That we have a corporate gifting policy, why we have it, and how they can abide by it
Why? So they're not unintentionally putting the company at risk	*Why?* To help employees avoid unintentionally putting the company at risk
Timing for when they need to know: Mid November, before holiday gifting starts	*Timing for when we want audiences to know:* Mid November, before holiday gifting starts

Why? Gifting will be top of mind at this time	*Why?* Gifting will be top of mind at this time
They need to: Understand and abide by the policy; report out-of-policy gifts to the compliance department	*We need them to:* Understand and abide by the policy; report out-of-policy gifts to the compliance department
Why? Do the right thing to protect the company	*Why?* Do the right thing to protect the company
Timing for when they need to take action: Mid November through the New Year	*Timing for when we want audiences to take action:* Mid November through the New Year
Why? That's the time period when gifts are most likely to be given and received	*Why?* That's the time period when gifts are most likely to be given and received
Benefits/What's in it for them: Still able to give and receive gifts within company policy	*Benefits/What's in it for us:* Ensure compliance with corporate gifting policy
Why? Employees enjoy giving and receiving gifts and may be accustomed to being able to do so	*Why?* Managing company risk by ensuring compliance with the corporate gifting policy

Audience #2: _____	
They care about:	We care about:
Why?	Why?
They need to know:	We want audiences to know:
Why?	Why?
Timing for when they need to know:	Timing for when we want audiences to know:
Why?	Why?
They need to do:	We want audiences to know:
Why?	Why?
Timing for when they need to take action:	Timing for when we want audiences to take action:
Why?	Why?
Benefits/What's in it for them:	Benefits/What's in it for us:
Why?	Why?

Audience #3:	
They care about:	*We care about:*
Why?	*Why?*
They need to know:	*We want audiences to know:*
Why?	*Why?*
Timing for when they need to know:	*Timing for when we want audiences to know:*
Why?	*Why?*
They need to do:	*We want audiences to know:*
Why?	*Why?*
Timing for when they need to take action:	*Timing for when we want audiences to take action:*
Why?	*Why?*
Benefits/What's in it for them:	*Benefits/What's in it for us:*
Why?	*Why?*

CONTENT CREATION CHECKLIST

Use this checklist to help you identify the critical ideas and information your communications must address.

Key facts that need to be communicated:
- [ ] Who
- [ ] What
- [ ] When
- [ ] Where
- [ ] Why

See previous worksheet:
- [ ] Wants by audience
- [ ] Needs by audience
- [ ] Timing "hook" by audience
- [ ] Actions the audience needs to take
- [ ] Benefits by audience
- [ ] Wants for compliance
- [ ] Needs for compliance
- [ ] Timing "hook" for compliance
- [ ] Actions compliance wants the audience to take
- [ ] Benefits for compliance

If not already covered above:
- [ ] Connection to company priorities or strategy
- [ ] Benefits/importance to those the company serves
- [ ] Any other relevant information

CONTENT APPROVAL CHECKLIST

Use this checklist to help you identify the people who need to review and approve your communication before it's published.

The Business *(the audiences you're communicating with)*	**Compliance**
First Round Approver *(usually the subject matter expert (SME) with whom you directly work to create the content)*	
☐ Name: ☐ Feedback incorporated ☐ Notes about the nature of the feedback:	☐ Name: ☐ Feedback incorporated ☐ Notes about the nature of the feedback:
Second Round Approver *(usually the SME's boss or a department head)*	
☐ Name: ☐ Feedback incorporated ☐ Notes about the nature of the feedback:	☐ Name: ☐ Feedback incorporated ☐ Notes about the nature of the feedback:
Final Approver *(usually a VP within the group)*	
☐ Name: ☐ Feedback incorporated ☐ Notes about the nature of the feedback:	☐ Name: ☐ Feedback incorporated ☐ Notes about the nature of the feedback:

CONTENT PUBLICATION CHECKLIST

Use this checklist to understand the required steps and lead time needed before your content reaches your intended audiences. Determine the lead time based on the items below, then work backward from your ideal content delivery date to create a timeline/schedule to manage the process in accordance with this timing.

Ideal Date for Content to Reach the Audience: _____

Required Steps and Associated Timing

- [ ] **Approval process:** _____ days

    Agree on turnaround times with all reviewers from the previous worksheet upfront to understand the total time you'll need to allow for approvals.

    - [ ] Key deadlines to note:

        ....

        ....

        ....

- [ ] **Publication process:** _____ days

    Work with corporate communications to understand publication timing and required lead times for getting content published in their channels. This could include:

    - [ ] Publication schedule for certain vehicles (e.g., newsletter distributed each Monday)
    - [ ] Content schedule for each vehicle—often called an editorial calendar (e.g., content for daily intranet updates are scheduled a month in advance except for urgent topics)
    - [ ] Time required by the communications team to edit your content as needed and schedule it in their systems for publication
    - [ ] Key deadlines to note:

        ....

        ....

        ....

☐ **Advance notice/pre-inform process:** _____ days

Determine which groups, if any, need to receive a copy of your content before it's shared with the broader audience of end users. This could include leadership teams in compliance and other involved departments, the executive team, etc.

    ☐ Groups to pre-inform and date for each:

    ....

    ....

    ....

☐ **Printing and/or shipping lead times:** _____ days

While fewer and fewer corporate materials are printed and shipped these days, take this into consideration if it applies to your situation (e.g., you're creating an article for distribution at an industry event). Work to understand the printer's deadline for receiving materials, their lead time for producing them, and how long it will take to ship.

    ☐ Key deadlines to note:

    ....

    ....

    ....

ONGOING VOICE OF THE CUSTOMER IDEAS

Complete this worksheet to establish what your audience wants and needs to understand from your communication, compared with what the compliance department wants and needs to communicate. Identify where those wants and needs align and where they diverge, and plan ahead for how to approach any issues you identify.

Existing Channels	Metrics by Channel *(quantitative and qualitative)*	Key Feedback
Comments/likes/shares on intranet articles		
Comments/likes/shares on internal or external social media *(e.g., Yammer, Jive, Twitter, LinkedIn)*		
Readership statistics for compliance content *(e.g., email open rates, link clickthroughs, time spent on webpages)*		

Other Possible Sources of Feedback

- Central mailbox for people to send questions or comments
- Q&A sessions during town halls, webinars, investor calls, etc.
- Feedback component in mobile apps
- Other: ....

Plans for monitoring the content/tone of feedback, and how compliance will respond:
....
....
....

New Ideas for Collecting Feedback

Items noted above that aren't available today but could be implemented:
....
....
....

Other ideas:
....
....
....

IDENTIFYING THE CORE CONCEPTS OF YOUR MESSAGE

Use this worksheet to identify the core concepts, or key facts, about your message—the details that won't change, regardless of who you're communicating with. Then, use the following worksheets to determine the variation needed based on audience, channel, and format.

Core Concepts

Who: ....

What: ....

When: ....

Where: ....

Why: ....

How: ....

PLANNING FOR REPETITION: AUDIENCE VARIATION

Use this worksheet to determine how you could create multiple messages about the same topic for the same audience, but with a different focus each time. The goal is to repeat the core content to help your audience retain it while focusing on various aspects of the content each time to keep it interesting. Repeat this exercise for each audience you're targeting if the message is different for each.

What are the key ideas to communicate to this audience about this topic?
....
....

What are the key dates or milestones? When will this topic impact this audience?
....
....

What are the key things the audience needs to know about why we're doing this?
....
....

What actions do I need my audience to take, and in what order?
....
....

Based on the above, what are a few different angles I could take to share the same information with the same audience in a varied way?

Angle 1: ....
Angle 2: ....
Angle 3: ....

PLANNING FOR REPETITION: CHANNEL AND FORMAT VARIATION

Use this worksheet to determine how you could create multiple messages about the same topic that vary by channel. The goal is to repeat the core content to help your audience retain it while sharing the message using varied channels to cut through the "noise" and reach your audience.

Refer to Chapter 4 to identify the right channels to use to reach your audience before you conduct this exercise.

The available channels to reach my audience (as identified in Chapter 4) are:

Channel 1: ....

Channel 2: ....

Channel 3: ....

Channel 4: ....

Channel 5: ....

For each of the above channels...

The length requirements or limitations are:

Channel 1: ....

Channel 2: ....

Channel 3: ....

Channel 4: ....

Channel 5: ....

Is there an opportunity to use audiovisual formats in addition to words? If so, what? What are the technical requirements or limitations associated with each?

Channel 1: ....

Channel 2: ....

Channel 3: ....

Channel 4: ....

Channel 5: ....

Based on the above, what are the different channels and formats I could use to share the same information with the same audience in a varied way?

Idea 1: ....

Idea 2: ....

Idea 3: ....

FEEDBACK: TRACKING DATA

Use this worksheet to track audience feedback from your communication, customizing as needed based on the previous planning worksheets.

INTERNAL CHANNELS

Channel	Metrics
Intranet	Avg. time spent on page: _____ Avg. time spent watching videos (as applicable): _____ Most clicked links: _____ _____ _____ Other: _____
Internal Social Media (e.g., Yammer)	Avg. # of likes: _____ Avg. # of comments: _____ Avg. # of shares/reshares: _____ Avg. time spent watching videos (as applicable): _____ Avg. # of link clicks: _____
Email	Avg. open rate: _____ Avg. clickthrough rate on links (as applicable): _____

EXTERNAL CHANNELS

Channel	Metrics
Website	Avg. time spent per page: _____ Avg. time spent watching videos (as applicable): _____ Avg. # of link clicks: _____ Other: _____
External Social Media (e.g., LinkedIn, Facebook)	Avg. # of likes: _____ Avg. # of comments: _____ Avg. # of shares/reshares: _____ Avg. time spent watching videos (as applicable): _____ Avg. # of link clicks: _____
Third-Party Publication	Media coverage - Tone of coverage (positive/neutral/negative): - Accuracy of coverage: - % of key messages published (i.e., how much of your desired message came through in the final article?): Blogs, other social media coverage - Tone of coverage (positive/neutral/negative): - Accuracy of coverage: - % of key messages published (i.e., how much of your desired message came through in the final article?):

PLANNING FOR FEEDBACK: RESPONSE PLAN

Use this worksheet to track audience feedback from your communication, customizing as needed based on your planning worksheet, above.

Assign a point person. Who has the most knowledge of this topic?

....

Establish monitoring frequency. Customize the below based on an agreed-upon schedule and use as a checklist for accomplishing the desired frequency.

Day 1
- ☐ Morning
- ☐ Midday
- ☐ End of day

Day 2
- ☐ Morning
- ☐ Midday
- ☐ End of day

Day 3
- ☐ Morning
- ☐ Midday
- ☐ End of day

Day 4
- ☐ Morning
- ☐ Midday
- ☐ End of day

Day 5
- ☐ Morning
- ☐ Midday
- ☐ End of day

Day 6
- ☐ Morning
- ☐ Midday
- ☐ End of day

Day 7
- ☐ Morning
- ☐ Midday
- ☐ End of day

Anticipate challenging responses.

Topic/sentiment: ....
How we'll handle: ....
Additional approver(s) before responding: ....

Topic/sentiment: ....
How we'll handle: ....
Additional approver(s) before responding: ....

Topic/sentiment: ....
How we'll handle: ....
Additional approver(s) before responding: ....

Monitor for trends in feedback.

Trend: ....
Response needed (if any): ....

Trend: ....
Response needed (if any): ....

Trend: ....
Response needed (if any): ....

GATHERING VOICE OF THE CUSTOMER FEEDBACK

Use this worksheet to detail how you'll gather feedback from voice of the customer stakeholders and where you need to further customize to meet your organization's unique needs.

What support are you looking for from the compliance program?
....
....
....

What words would you use to describe the compliance program?
....
....
....

In what areas does compliance really excel? In what areas can the compliance program improve?
....
....
....

What's your biggest complaint about compliance?
....
....
....

What should compliance keep/stop/start doing?
Keep: ....
Stop: ....
Start: ....

CCI Press is the publishing imprint of CCI Media Group, parent company of Corporate Compliance Insights (CCI). CCI is the web's premier, independent, global source of news and opinion for compliance, ethics, risk, and audit. Founded in 2010, CCI provides a knowledge-sharing forum and publishing platform for established and emerging voices in compliance and ethics, and is a recognized creator, publisher, and syndication source for editorial and multimedia content for today's compliance professional.

Made in the USA
Monee, IL
09 September 2021